Copyright © 2024 by Maxwell Williams

All rights reserved. No part of this publication may be reproduced, distributed, or transmitted in any form or by any means, including photocopying, recording, or other electronic or mechanical methods, without the prior written permission of the publisher, except in the case of brief quotations embodied in critical reviews and certain other non-commercial uses permitted by copyright law.

MySQL Queries

30-Day Crash Course for WordPress

BY

Maxwell Williams

Unleash the Power of Your WordPress Database: Master MySQL Queries in 30 Days!

Struggling to wrangle your WordPress website's database? Wish you could speak the language and unlock its full potential? Look no further! **MySQL Queries: 30-Day Crash Course for WordPress** is your comprehensive guide to mastering the art of querying your WordPress database in just one month.

Who is this book for?

- **WordPress Website Owners:** Take control of your website's data! This book empowers you to optimize performance, troubleshoot issues, and extract valuable insights from your database, even with no prior coding experience.
- **Content Creators and Marketers:** Fuel your content strategy with data-driven insights. Learn how to query your database to understand user behavior, identify popular content, and optimize your website for better engagement.
- **Freelancers and Designers:** Offer a valuable edge to your clients! This book equips you with the skills to manage and optimize WordPress databases for a wider range of projects.

Why is this book profitable for you?

- **Save Time and Money:** No more relying on expensive developers for basic database tasks. Learn to handle queries yourself and streamline your workflow.
- **Boost Website Performance:** Uncover hidden bottlenecks and optimize your database for lightning-fast loading times, leading to happier visitors and potentially improved search engine ranking.
- **Gain Valuable Data Insights:** Unlock the goldmine of information within your database. Learn to generate reports, track user behavior, and make data-driven decisions to enhance your website's effectiveness.
- **Future-Proof Your Skills:** Mastering MySQL queries is a valuable asset in the WordPress world. This skillset opens doors to new opportunities and positions you as a more competent website owner or developer.

What will you learn in 30 days?

This book takes you on a guided journey through the world of MySQL queries, specifically tailored for WordPress users:

- **The Fundamentals:** Grasp the core concepts of relational databases, understand the structure of your WordPress database, and explore the building blocks of queries.
- **Crafting Queries:** Learn how to write SELECT statements to retrieve specific data from your

database, filter results based on criteria, and sort data for better organization.
- **Data Manipulation:** Master the art of inserting, updating, and deleting data within your database, empowering you to maintain accurate and up-to-date information.
- **Advanced Techniques:** Delve deeper into JOINs, explore functions for data manipulation and analysis, and unlock the power of subqueries for complex data retrieval.
- **Performance Optimization:** Discover strategies to streamline queries, optimize database structure, and ensure your website runs at peak performance.
- **Security Essentials:** Learn best practices for safeguarding your database from unauthorized access and potential security threats.
- **Real-World Examples:** Throughout the book, practical examples relevant to WordPress website management scenarios are provided to solidify your understanding.

By the end of this 30-day crash course, you'll be wielding MySQL queries with confidence, transforming your relationship with your WordPress database from frustration to empowerment!

Contents

CHAPTER 1: INTRODUCTION TO MYSQL AND DATABASES 6

   1.1 What is a Database and Why Do You Need It? 10

   1.2 Introducing SQL: The Language of Databases 12

   1.3 MySQL for WordPress: A Powerful Combination 13

   Project: Install and Set Up a Local Database Environment for WordPress development. 18

CHAPTER 2: GETTING STARTED WITH PHPMYADMIN 23

   2.1 Exploring the phpMyAdmin Interface: A Quick Tour 23

   2.2 Viewing, Editing, and Deleting Data in WordPress Tables 26

   23. Importing and Exporting Your Database for Backup and Migration 29

   Project: Familiarize yourself with phpMyAdmin by exploring your WordPress database tables. 33

CHAPTER 3: ESSENTIAL MYSQL QUERY TYPES 36

   3.1 Selecting Data: The Power of the `SELECT` statement 36

   3.2 Filtering Your Data with `WHERE` Clauses 39

   3.3 Sorting and Ordering Results with `ORDER BY` 43

   Project: Write basic `SELECT` queries to retrieve specific data from your WordPress database. 47

CHAPTER 4: WORKING WITH JOINS IN WORDPRESS 52

   4.1 Demystifying Joins: Connecting Tables in Your Database . 52

   4.2 Different Types of Joins: `INNER JOIN`, `LEFT JOIN`, and More 55

4.3 Using Joins to Retrieve Related Data in WordPress (e.g., Posts and Comments) 60

Project: Practice writing queries using joins to retrieve data from multiple WordPress tables. 63

CHAPTER 5: OPTIMIZING QUERIES FOR FASTER PERFORMANCE 67

5.1 Understanding Query Performance: Identifying Slow Queries 67

5.2 Indexing Strategies: Supercharge Your Database Searches 71

5.3 Writing Optimized Queries: Best Practices to Avoid Bottlenecks 74

Project: Analyze slow queries in your WordPress environment and optimize them for better performance. 78

CHAPTER 6: WORKING WITH USERS AND USER DATA ... 83

6.1 Exploring the `wp_users` Table: Understanding User Data Structure 83

6.1 Exploring the `wp_users` Table: Understanding User Data Structure 83

6.2 Retrieving Specific User Information with Targeted Queries 86

6.3 Managing Users and User Roles through Database Actions 91

Project: Write queries to retrieve specific user information and practice basic user management through the database 95

CHAPTER 7: CUSTOM POST TYPES AND DATA MANAGEMENT 99

7.1 Unveiling Custom Post Type Tables: Structure and Data Storage 99

7.2 Querying Custom Post Type Data with Tailored Statements 102

7.3 Filtering and Sorting Custom Post Types for Specific Needs 107

7.4 Creating a Custom Loop to Display Filtered and Sorted Recipes 110

Project: Write queries to retrieve and manipulate data from custom post types in your WordPress site. 113

CHAPTER 8: LEVERAGING DATABASE VIEWS FOR SIMPLIFIED QUERIES 118

8.1 What are Database Views? Benefits and Use Cases for WordPress 118

8.2 Creating and Managing Database Views for Common Queries 122

8.3 Using Views to Simplify Complex Data Retrieval Operations 128

Project: Create a database view for a frequently used complex query in your WordPress environment. 131

CHAPTER 9: SECURITY CONSIDERATIONS FOR DATABASE ACCESS 137

9.1 Understanding User Privileges and Access Control in MySQL 141

9.2 Securing Your Database Connection: Best Practices for Usernames and Passwords 144

9.3 Ongoing Maintenance: Keeping Your WordPress Database Secure 148

Chapter 10: Advanced Techniques and Resources for WordPress Database Optimization 151

CHAPTER 11: Performance Optimization Beyond the Database: 156

    What is Server-Side Caching? 157

    Benefits of Server-Side Caching: 157

    How Does Server-Side Caching Work? 157

    Enabling Server-Side Caching: 158

    11.2 Code Optimization: 160

    Understanding Code Optimization: 160

    Optimizing Your WordPress Code: 160

    1. Minification: 160

    2. Code Splitting: 161

    3. Leverage Browser Caching: 161

    4. Database Optimization: 162

    5. Lazy Loading: 162

    11.3 Image Optimization: 164

    Content Delivery Network (CDN): 167

        How Does a CDN Work with WordPress? 168

        Things to Consider When Using a CDN: 169

        Popular CDN Providers: 170

CHAPTER 1: INTRODUCTION TO MYSQL AND DATABASES

Learning Objectives:

- Grasp the fundamentals of databases, SQL, and MySQL.
- Understand how they work together to power your WordPress website.

This chapter lays the foundation for your MySQL adventure. We'll explore the concept of databases, the language they use (SQL), and how MySQL fits into the WordPress ecosystem. Whether you're a complete beginner or a seasoned developer, this chapter will ensure you have the essential knowledge to navigate the world of WordPress databases.

What is a Database?

Imagine a library – a vast collection of information neatly organized in bookshelves. A database functions similarly, storing and managing information electronically. Instead of books, it uses tables with rows and columns to categorize and store data efficiently.

1.2 Introducing SQL: The Database Language

Think of SQL (Structured Query Language) as the librarian's assistant. Just as the assistant helps you find specific books, SQL allows you to interact with the database. It provides commands to retrieve, modify, and manage the information stored within.

SQL, which stands for Structured Query Language, is the cornerstone of communication with relational databases. It's a standardized language used to interact with, manipulate, and retrieve data stored in these databases. Whether you're a complete beginner or a seasoned developer, understanding SQL unlocks the power of managing and analyzing your data effectively.

Think of SQL as a special set of instructions you give to the database. These instructions tell the database what information you need, how to filter it, and how to organize it for your specific purposes. Just like you use English to communicate with others, you use SQL to "talk" to your database.

Here are some key concepts in SQL:

Databases: Organized collections of data structured in tables. Each table has rows (records) and columns (fields) that define the data being stored.

Tables: Think of them like spreadsheets where each row represents a unique record, and each column represents a specific data point within that record (e.g., a product table might have rows for each product, with columns for product name, price, and description).

Queries: Specific requests you make to the database using SQL statements. These statements tell the database what data to retrieve or manipulate.

Imagine you run an online store and want to find all orders placed in the last month. Here's a basic SQL query to achieve that:

```sql
SELECT
FROM orders
WHERE order_date >= DATE_SUB(CURDATE(), INTERVAL 1 MONTH);
```

`SELECT `: This retrieves all columns (fields) from the table.

`FROM orders`: This specifies the table you want to query (the orders table in this case).

`WHERE order_date >= DATE_SUB(CURDATE(), INTERVAL 1 MONTH)`: This filters the results to only include orders placed within the last month.

`CURDATE()`: This function returns the current date.

`DATE_SUB(CURDATE(), INTERVAL 1 MONTH)`: This subtracts one month from the current date to get the starting date for the filter.

This is a very simple example, but it demonstrates the basic structure of an SQL query. As you progress, you'll learn more complex commands to perform a variety of tasks on your database.

Benefits of Using SQL:

Standardized language: Works across different database platforms with minor variations.

Powerful and flexible: Allows you to retrieve, modify, analyze, and manage data efficiently.

Essential for data-driven applications: Core technology behind many modern web applications.

1.3 MySQL: The Powerful Engine for WordPress

Now, let's bring WordPress into the picture. MySQL is a popular database management system, like a powerful software program, that acts as the library itself. It houses your WordPress data, including posts, comments, user information, and more. SQL acts as the intermediary, allowing you to communicate with and manipulate your data in MySQL.

By understanding these core concepts, you'll be well on your way to unlocking the potential of MySQL queries for optimizing your WordPress website.

Ready to dive deeper? The next sections will explore these concepts further and equip you with the practical skills to manage your WordPress database.

1.1 What is a Database and Why Do You Need It?

In the digital world, data is king. Every website, app, and online service relies on data to function. But managing large amounts of information can be a nightmare if it's scattered across different files or folders. That's where databases come in.

Think of a database as a giant organized filing cabinet. It stores information in a structured way, making it easy to add, retrieve, and manage data. Here's a breakdown:

Structured Data: Instead of random text files, databases store information in tables with rows and columns. Each row represents a single record (like a specific customer), and each column represents a specific piece of information about that record (e.g., name, email address).

Easy Retrieval: Imagine searching for a specific customer in a cluttered filing cabinet versus a well-organized one with labeled folders. Databases allow you to quickly find data using queries, which are like search instructions telling the database what you're looking for.

Why Use a Database for WordPress?

Even a simple WordPress website generates data – posts, comments, user information, etc. As your website grows, managing this data manually becomes impractical. A database offers several benefits:

1. Organization: No more hunting through text files or spreadsheets. Databases keep your data organized and easily accessible.

2. Efficiency: Searching and retrieving data becomes a breeze with queries. You can find specific information quickly, saving time and effort.
3. Scalability: As your website grows, the database can easily scale to accommodate more data without performance issues.
4. Data Integrity: Databases ensure consistency and accuracy of your data. Unlike individual files, any changes made to data in a database are reflected everywhere it's used.

Here's a simple example: Imagine a basic blog with just a few posts. Initially, you might have a text file listing each post's title and content. But as you add more posts, managing this data becomes cumbersome. A database, on the other hand, would have a table with separate columns for post title, content, author, and publication date. This allows you to easily add new posts, search for specific ones, and even sort them by date or author.

1.2 Introducing SQL: The Language of Databases

Imagine a massive library filled with information, neatly organized into sections, shelves, and books. This is essentially what a database is – a structured collection of data. But unlike a library, you need a special language to access and manipulate this information. That's where SQL (pronounced "ess-que-el") comes in.

SQL stands for Structured Query Language. It's a standardized language used to interact with relational databases, which are the most common type of database used today. Relational databases store data in tables, with rows and columns. Think of a table like a spreadsheet – rows represent individual entries, and columns represent specific categories of information within those entries.

Here's a simple example:

Customer ID	Name	Email
1	John Smith	Joh@gmail.com
2	Jane Doe	Ja@gmail.com
3	Mike Jones	Mi@gmail.com

This table might represent customer information in a database.

SQL allows you to interact with this data in various ways:

Retrieve data: You can use SQL to select specific information from tables, like finding all customers with emails ending in "@example.com".

Insert data: You can add new entries (rows) to your tables, like adding a new customer.

Update data: You can modify existing data in your tables, like updating a customer's email address.

Delete data: You can remove entries from your tables when necessary.

Key Takeaways:

Databases store information in a structured way.

SQL is the language used to interact with relational databases.

SQL allows you to retrieve, insert, update, and delete data.

SQL is a valuable skill for both beginners and experienced developers.

1.3 MySQL for WordPress: A Powerful Combination

MySQL and WordPress form a powerful partnership that drives millions of websites across the globe. In this section, we'll explore why this combination is so effective and how it benefits both beginners and experienced developers.

What is MySQL?

MySQL is a popular open-source relational database management system (RDBMS). It's essentially a software application that allows you to store, organize, and access data in a structured format. Imagine your website's content (posts, pages, comments) as pieces of information stored in a filing cabinet. MySQL acts as that filing cabinet, keeping everything organized and easily retrievable.

How Does MySQL Work with WordPress?

Behind the scenes of your WordPress website lies a powerful database management system called MySQL. It acts as the central storage unit for all your website's crucial information, from blog posts and comments to user accounts and settings. Here's a breakdown of how MySQL interacts with WordPress:

1. Data Storage:

Imagine your website content – posts, pages, comments – as pieces of information. MySQL stores this data in a structured format, using tables with rows and columns. Each table represents a specific type of data, like "posts" or "users." Rows within a table hold individual entries, and columns define the characteristics of those entries (e.g., post title, author, content).

For example, the "posts" table might have one row for each blog post on your site. Each row would have columns for the post title, content, author ID (linking to the "users" table), and publication date.

2. Communication via PHP:

WordPress itself doesn't directly interact with MySQL. It relies on a programming language called PHP to bridge the gap. Here's how it works:

When a user visits your website and requests a specific page, WordPress uses PHP to create a query. This query is a set of instructions written in a special language called SQL (Structured Query Language) that tells MySQL what data to retrieve.

The PHP code sends the SQL query to the MySQL server.

MySQL receives the query, understands its instructions, and retrieves the relevant data from the database tables.

MySQL sends the requested data back to the PHP code.

Finally, PHP processes the retrieved data and uses it to dynamically generate the web page content you see in your browser.

Think of PHP as a translator – it takes human-readable instructions from WordPress and converts them into a language that MySQL understands. Once MySQL provides the data, PHP translates it back into a format that your web browser can display.

Here's a simplified example of an SQL query (SELECT statement) written in PHP:

```php
$sql = "SELECT FROM posts WHERE post_status = 'publish'";
$result = $wpdb->get_results($sql);

// Process and display the retrieved posts using $result data
```

This code snippet retrieves all published posts ("post_status = 'publish'") from the "posts" table and stores the results in the

`$result` variable. WordPress can then use this data to display the posts on your website.

3. Dynamic and Efficient:

This communication between WordPress, PHP, and MySQL allows for a dynamic website experience. Every time a user visits a page or interacts with your site, a tailored query can be sent to the database, retrieving the most up-to-date information. This is why your website can display different content to different users based on their login status or browsing preferences.

Key Takeaways:

MySQL is the database management system that stores all your WordPress website's data in a structured format.

WordPress uses PHP to communicate with MySQL using SQL queries.

This collaboration allows for dynamic and efficient website functionality, retrieving and displaying relevant data on demand.

Benefits for Beginners:

Easy to Use: WordPress provides a user-friendly interface for managing your website content without needing to directly interact with the database. You can create posts, edit pages, and manage users without writing complex code.

Scalability: As your website grows and accumulates more data, MySQL can seamlessly scale to accommodate the increased storage needs. You won't need to worry about your database becoming overloaded.

Benefits for Experienced Developers:

1. Direct Database Access: For advanced customization or plugin development, experienced developers can access and manipulate the underlying WordPress data stored in MySQL using PHP. This allows for building powerful functionalities and features.
2. Performance Optimization: With a solid understanding of MySQL, developers can optimize database queries, ensuring your website retrieves information efficiently and delivers fast loading times.

MySQL serves as the backbone for storing and managing your website's data, while WordPress provides a user-friendly interface for creating and managing your content. This powerful partnership caters to both beginners and developers, offering a user-friendly experience for content creation and the flexibility for advanced customization.

Let's consider an example. When you create a new blog post in WordPress, the title, content, and other details are stored in specific tables within the MySQL database. When someone visits your website and views that post, WordPress retrieves the relevant data from the database and displays it on the page.

Project: Install and Set Up a Local Database Environment for WordPress development.

Developing a WordPress website often involves testing and tweaking features before deploying them live. To avoid affecting your existing website, it's recommended to create a local development environment. This environment mirrors a live server, allowing you to work on your WordPress site locally on your computer.

A crucial component of any WordPress installation is the database. This is where WordPress stores all its data, including posts, comments, user information, and website settings. In this guide, we'll walk you through setting up a local database environment specifically for WordPress development.

There are several ways to achieve this, but we'll focus on using a popular tool called XAMPP. XAMPP is a free and open-source software package that bundles essential components like Apache web server, MySQL database server, and PHP (a programming language used by WordPress) into a single installation.

Here's what you'll need:

A computer with a decent internet connection

XAMPP installer for your operating system (Windows, Mac, or Linux) - You can download it from the official XAMPP website: https://www.apachefriends.org/download.html

Steps:

1. Download and Install XAMPP:

Head over to the XAMPP download page and choose the installer compatible with your operating system.

Once downloaded, run the installer and follow the on-screen instructions. It's generally recommended to keep the default installation settings unless you have specific requirements.

2. Start the Apache and MySQL Services:

Open the XAMPP Control Panel, which should automatically launch after installation.

Click the "Start" buttons next to the "Apache" and "MySQL" services. These buttons will turn green when the services are running.

3. Create a Database for WordPress:

We'll use a web interface called phpMyAdmin to manage our MySQL database. In most cases, you can access it by opening http://localhost/phpmyadmin in your web browser.

Note: "localhost" refers to your own computer, and "phpmyadmin" is the default directory for phpMyAdmin within XAMPP.

You might be prompted for a username and password. By default, XAMPP uses "root" for the username and leaves the password field blank.

4. Creating the Database:

Once logged into phpMyAdmin, you'll see a list of databases on the left-hand side.

Click on the "New" tab to create a new database.

Enter a name for your database (e.g., "my_wordpress_site"). This name will be used by WordPress to store its data.

Click the "Create" button to create the database.

5. Download and Extract WordPress Files:

Download the latest version of WordPress from the official website:
https://wordpress.org/download/

Extract the downloaded zip file to a folder on your computer. This folder will contain all the WordPress core files.

6. Copy WordPress Files to Document Root:

By default, XAMPP uses the "htdocs" folder as its document root. This is the directory where web server files are stored and made accessible through a web browser.

Open your file explorer and navigate to the folder where you extracted the WordPress files.

Copy all the extracted files and folders into the "htdocs" folder within your XAMPP installation directory.

7. Configure WordPress with Database Details:

Open your web browser and navigate to http://localhost/your_wordpress_folder (replace "your_wordpress_folder" with the actual name of the folder where you copied the WordPress files).

This will launch the WordPress installation wizard.

Follow the on-screen instructions, providing details such as your website title, username, and password.

Crucially, in the "Database Settings" section, you'll need to enter the following information:

Database Name: The name you chose for your database in step 4 (e.g., "my_wordpress_site").

Username: By default, XAMPP uses "root" for the username.

Password: Leave this blank if you didn't set a password for the MySQL service in XAMPP.

Database Host: In most cases, you can leave this as "localhost".

8. Complete the Installation:

Once you've entered the database details, click the "Install WordPress" button.

WordPress will complete the installation process and create the necessary tables within your database.

You've now successfully set up a local database environment for WordPress development. You can access your WordPress admin

CHAPTER 2: GETTING STARTED WITH PHPMYADMIN

Learning Objectives: Master navigating and managing your WordPress database using phpMyAdmin.

2.1 Exploring the phpMyAdmin Interface: A Quick Tour

Welcome to your first steps in managing your WordPress database! phpMyAdmin is a web-based interface that acts as a user-friendly control panel for your MySQL database. It allows you to view, edit, and manipulate data within your WordPress installation, eliminating the need for complex command-line tools.

Navigating the Interface:

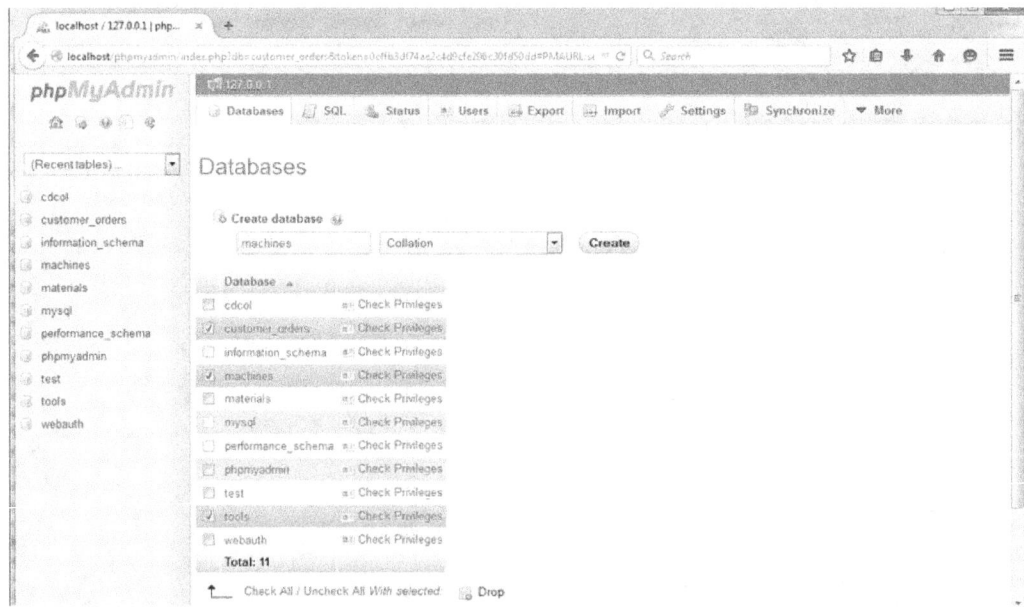

Upon logging into phpMyAdmin, you'll be greeted with a well-organized layout. Here's a breakdown of some key elements:

Left-hand Panel: This panel lists all the databases on your server. The database containing your WordPress data will typically have a prefix like "wp_" (e.g., "wp_posts," "wp_users"). Clicking on a database name expands it to reveal all the tables within that database.

Central Panel: This area displays information about the currently selected database or table. Depending on your selection, you might see a list of tables, table structure, or query results.

Top Navigation Bar: This bar provides various functions, including options to create new databases, import/export data, and manage user privileges (more advanced).

Understanding Key Terms:

Database: A structured collection of data organized into tables. Think of it like a filing cabinet with labeled folders (tables) containing specific information (data).

Table: A fundamental unit of data storage within a database. Each table has rows and columns, similar to a spreadsheet.

Row: A horizontal record in a table representing a single data entry. In WordPress, a row in the "wp_posts" table might represent a single blog post with its title, content, and author information.

Column: A vertical field in a table defining a specific attribute of the data. In the "wp_posts" table example, columns might include "post_title," "post_content," and "post_author_id."

Exploring Tables:

Once you click on your WordPress database name, you'll see a list of tables. Some common WordPress tables include:

`wp_posts`: Stores information about your blog posts, pages, and revisions.

`wp_users`: Contains user data like usernames, passwords (hashed for security), and email addresses.

`wp_comments`: Holds information about comments left on your blog posts.

Performing Basic Actions:

Viewing Table Data: Clicking on a table name displays its structure (columns) and allows you to browse actual data entries (rows). You can navigate through pages of data or search for specific entries using the search bar.

Editing Data: phpMyAdmin allows basic editing of individual data entries within a table. However, be cautious when editing, as changes can potentially affect your website functionality.

Writing queries to retrieve specific data from your WordPress database.

Importing and exporting data for backup or migration purposes.

Understanding table structure and relationships for complex queries.

PhpMyAdmin serves as a powerful tool for managing your WordPress database. However, always exercise caution and back up your database before making significant changes. The next sections will delve deeper into specific actions you can perform with phpMyAdmin to optimize your WordPress experience.

2.2 Viewing, Editing, and Deleting Data in WordPress Tables

Now that you're familiar with the phpMyAdmin interface, let's explore how to interact with the data stored in your WordPress tables.

Viewing Data:

Navigating to Tables: Within phpMyAdmin, locate your WordPress database name on the left panel and click on it. This will reveal a list of tables within that database.

Selecting a Table: Choose the table you want to view. Common WordPress tables include "wp_posts" (stores blog posts), "wp_users" (holds user information), and "wp_comments" (contains comments).

Browsing Data: Clicking on a table name displays its structure (columns) and allows you to view the actual data entries (rows).

You'll see a grid-like layout with column headers representing data fields and each row holding information for a specific entry.

Pagination and Search: Most tables are paginated, meaning you can navigate through multiple pages of data entries using the controls at the bottom. Additionally, some tables might offer a search bar allowing you to filter data based on specific keywords.

Imagine you want to view a specific blog post in the "wp_posts" table. You'd navigate to the "wp_posts" table, and each row would represent a different post. Columns might include "ID" (unique identifier for each post), "post_title" (title of the post), "post_content" (content of the post), and "post_author_id" (ID of the author). You could then scroll through the rows to find the specific post you're interested in.

Editing Data (Caution Advised):

While phpMyAdmin allows basic editing of individual data entries, exercise extreme caution! Incorrect edits can potentially break your website functionality. It's generally recommended to edit data through the WordPress interface itself whenever possible.

Locating the Entry: Locate the specific row representing the data you want to edit. Click on the pencil icon next to the desired field within that row.

Modifying the Value: A small edit box will appear. Carefully enter the new value you want to update and click "Go" to save the changes.

Deleting Data

Deleting data is even more sensitive than editing. Accidental deletion can seriously affect your website. It's strongly recommended to back up your database before attempting any deletions.

Selecting the Entry: Locate the row you want to delete. Check the checkbox next to it.

Confirming Deletion: With the checkbox selected, scroll up to the "With selected:" dropdown menu at the top and choose "Delete." A confirmation window will appear. Double-check your selection before clicking "Yes" to permanently delete the data.

Note:

Editing and deleting data in phpMyAdmin should be done with caution and a backup in place.

For most tasks, modifying data through the WordPress interface itself is safer and more user-friendly.

The next section will dive deeper into a more powerful technique - writing MySQL queries - to retrieve and manipulate data from your WordPress database.

23. Importing and Exporting Your Database for Backup and Migration

Imagine your WordPress website as a bustling city. Your database holds all the crucial information – the blog posts, user accounts, comments, and settings – just like the city's libraries, archives, and citizen records. Keeping backups is essential, just like having a contingency plan for the city. This section will explore how to import and export your WordPress database using phpMyAdmin, a valuable tool for both backups and migrations.

Understanding Backups and Migrations:

Backup: Creating a copy of your database at a specific point in time. This acts as a safety net in case of accidental data loss or website issues. Regularly backing up your database ensures you can restore it to a previous working state.

Migration: Moving your entire WordPress installation, including the database, to a new server or hosting provider. This process often involves exporting the database from the old server and importing it into the new one.

Importing and Exporting with phpMyAdmin:

Exporting Your Database:

1. Log in to phpMyAdmin: Use the credentials provided by your web hosting service (refer to Chapter 2.1 for guidance).

2. Select Your Database: In the left-hand panel, locate your WordPress database (usually with a prefix like "wp_"). Click on it to expand and reveal the tables within.

3. Export Options: Locate the "Export" tab at the top of the phpMyAdmin interface. Here, you can choose the format for your exported data (usually "SQL"). You can also select specific tables to export if needed.

4. Start Export: Click the "Go" button at the bottom of the page to initiate the export process. phpMyAdmin will download a compressed file containing your database data.

Importing Your Database:

1. Access phpMyAdmin on Your New Location: If you're performing a migration, access phpMyAdmin on your new server or hosting provider.

2. Select the Database: Choose the target database where you want to import your data (ensure it's empty or compatible with your WordPress installation).

3. Import Options: Navigate to the "Import" tab. Click the "Browse" button and select the exported SQL file from your previous step.

4. Import Confirmation: Click the "Go" button to start the import process. phpMyAdmin will read the SQL file and insert the data into your new database.

Note:

Security: Always back up your database before performing any significant changes or migrations.

Compatibility: When migrating, ensure the new server environment is compatible with your WordPress version and database requirements.

Advanced Options: phpMyAdmin offers various export/import options for advanced users. This section focused on the basic functionalities. Refer to phpMyAdmin documentation for detailed explanations of all available settings.

Additional Considerations for Importing and Exporting:

File Size Limitations: Some web hosting providers might have limitations on upload file sizes. If your exported database file is too large, you might need to compress it further (e.g., using tools like WinRAR or 7-Zip) before uploading.

Database Optimization (Optional): Before importing a large database, consider optimizing the tables using phpMyAdmin's optimization tools. This can improve performance on the new server.

Security: When downloading or uploading your database backup file, ensure you're using a secure connection (HTTPS) and avoid storing sensitive information like passwords in plain text within the database itself.

Alternative Backup Methods:

While phpMyAdmin offers a convenient way to manage your database, here are some alternative backup methods to consider:

Web Hosting Backups: Many web hosting providers offer automatic backups as part of their service. Check with your web host to see if they offer database backups and how to access them if needed.

Backup Plugins: Numerous WordPress plugins can automate database backups and store them securely in cloud storage services like Dropbox or Google Drive.

Having multiple backup options provides an extra layer of security for your valuable website data.

Project: Familiarize yourself with phpMyAdmin by exploring your WordPress database tables.

Time to get your hands dirty! In this project, you'll delve into your WordPress database using phpMyAdmin. Remember, we covered logging into phpMyAdmin in Chapter 2.1. Now, let's explore the treasures (data) it holds!

1. Locating Your WordPress Database:

Once logged into phpMyAdmin, look for the left-hand panel. This section lists all the databases on your server.

Your WordPress database will typically have a prefix like "wp_". For example, it might be named "wp_myblog" or "wp_12345" (depending on your setup).

2. Exploring Your Database Tables:

Click on your WordPress database name in the left-hand panel. This will expand it to reveal a list of tables within that database.

[Imagen of phpMyAdmin interface with database tables list expanded]

Common WordPress tables include:

`wp_posts`: Stores information about your blog posts, pages, and revisions.

`wp_users`: Contains user data like usernames, passwords (hashed for security), and email addresses.

`wp_comments`: Holds information about comments left on your blog posts.

There might be other tables depending on the plugins you have installed on your WordPress site.

3. Taking a Closer Look:

Click on a table name (e.g., `wp_posts`) to see its structure. This displays the columns (fields) that define the data stored in each row (record).

Each column represents a specific piece of information. For example, in the `wp_posts` table, you might see columns like:

`ID`: Unique identifier for each post.

`post_title`: Title of the post.

`post_content`: Main content of the post.

`post_author_id`: ID of the user who authored the post.

4. Browsing Data (Optional):

phpMyAdmin allows you to browse actual data entries (rows) within a table. Click the "Browse" tab at the top of the page.

You might see a paginated view of the data, allowing you to navigate through entries.

Important Note:

Be cautious when editing data directly within phpMyAdmin, especially for core WordPress tables. Accidental changes can potentially affect your website functionality. It's recommended to back up your database before making any modifications.

CHAPTER 3: ESSENTIAL MYSQL QUERY TYPES

Learning Objectives: Grasp the most commonly used MySQL query types for WordPress.

3.1 Selecting Data: The Power of the `SELECT` statement

In the world of WordPress and MySQL, the `SELECT` statement is your key to unlocking the treasures hidden within your database. Just like a librarian retrieves specific books from a vast collection, `SELECT` allows you to extract targeted data from your WordPress database.

Understanding the Basics:

What is a Query? A query is a question you ask the database. It tells the database what information you need and in what format.

The Power of `SELECT`: The `SELECT` statement forms the foundation of most database interactions. It allows you to retrieve specific data from one or more tables within your database.

Constructing a Basic `SELECT` Query:

The following structure represents a fundamental `SELECT` query:

```sql
SELECT column1, column2, ...
FROM table_name;
```

`SELECT`: This keyword initiates the query, indicating you want to retrieve data.

`column1, column2, ...`: This comma-separated list specifies the columns (fields) you want to retrieve from the table. You can select all columns using `*` (asterisk).

`FROM`: This keyword specifies the table name from which you want to extract data. Remember, your WordPress database consists of multiple tables, each storing specific information (e.g., posts, users, comments).

`;`: The semicolon marks the end of the query.

Example: Retrieving All Posts from the `wp_posts` Table:

Let's say you want to retrieve all posts from your WordPress database. Here's a basic query to achieve this:

```sql
SELECT
```

```
FROM wp_posts;
```

This query instructs the database to:

1. Use the `SELECT` statement.

2. Retrieve all columns (`` ` ``) from the table named `wp_posts`.

Running this query in phpMyAdmin or a similar tool will display a list of all your blog posts, including their titles, content, and other details stored in the `wp_posts` table.

Key Takeaways:

The `SELECT` statement is your primary tool for extracting data from your WordPress database.

By specifying columns and tables, you can target specific information.

Understanding the basic structure empowers you to construct more complex queries as needed.

3.2 Filtering Your Data with `WHERE` Clauses

Imagine you have a massive library full of books. But you only care about finding science fiction novels published after 2020. The WHERE clause in MySQL acts like a powerful filtering tool, allowing you to pinpoint specific data within your WordPress database based on defined conditions.

Understanding the WHERE Clause:

The WHERE clause is a core component of the SELECT statement, which is the primary way to retrieve data from your database. It lets you specify criteria that the data must meet to be included in the results.

Basic Structure:

SQL

SELECT *

FROM table_name

WHERE column_name = value;

SELECT *: This retrieves all columns (fields) from the specified table. You can also specify individual columns instead of "*".

FROM table_name: Replace "table_name" with the actual name of the table you want to query (e.g., "wp_posts" for blog posts).

WHERE column_name = value: This is where the filtering happens. You define a condition using a column name, a comparison operator (=, >, <, etc.), and a specific value to match.

Example: Filtering Posts by Category

Let's say you want to retrieve all blog posts from your WordPress site that belong to the "Science Fiction" category. Here's the query:

SQL

SELECT *

```
FROM wp_posts
WHERE post_category = 'Science Fiction';
```

In this example:

We're selecting all columns (`*`) from the `wp_posts` table.

The `WHERE` clause specifies that we only want posts where the `post_category` column value is exactly equal to `"Science Fiction"` (don't forget the single quotes for string values).

Running the Query:

You can execute these queries directly within phpMyAdmin's SQL query box. Simply paste the code, click "Go," and phpMyAdmin will display the results matching your criteria.

Common Comparison Operators:

`=` (Equal to)

`!=` (Not equal to)

`>` (Greater than)

`<` (Less than)

`>=` (Greater than or equal to)

`<=` (Less than or equal to)

Filtering with Multiple Conditions:

You can combine multiple `WHERE` clauses using logical operators like `AND` and `OR` to create more complex filters.

SQL

```
SELECT *
FROM wp_posts
WHERE post_category = 'Science Fiction' AND post_status = 'publish';
```

This query retrieves posts that are both in the "Science Fiction" category and have a publish status (drafts would be excluded).

Filtering with Text Data:

When filtering text data (like post titles), you need to enclose the value in single quotes:

SQL

```
SELECT *
FROM wp_posts
WHERE post_title LIKE '%alien%';
```

This query retrieves posts where the `post_title` column contains the word "alien" anywhere within the title (using the `LIKE` operator with a wildcard symbol `%`).

Mastering the WHERE Clause:

By understanding and practicing the `WHERE` clause, you can effectively target specific data within your WordPress database.

This empowers you to create more focused queries, analyze subsets of your data, and manage your website content with greater precision.

Experiment with different WHERE clause variations to refine your filtering criteria.

Refer to the MySQL documentation for a complete list of comparison operators and filtering functions.

Start with simple queries and gradually build your confidence in crafting more complex filters.

As you progress through this book, you'll discover even more powerful ways to leverage the WHERE clause in conjunction with other query elements for advanced data retrieval from your WordPress database

3.3 Sorting and Ordering Results with `ORDER BY`

Imagine you have a bookshelf overflowing with books on various topics. But they're all jumbled up! The `ORDER BY` clause in MySQL acts like a librarian, sorting your retrieved data in a specific order, making it easier to find what you need.

Understanding `ORDER BY`:

The `ORDER BY` clause is used within the `SELECT` statement to arrange your retrieved data based on a particular column. You can sort data in ascending order (A-Z, lowest to highest) or descending order (Z-A, highest to lowest).

Basic Syntax:

```sql
SELECT column1, column2, ...
FROM table_name
ORDER BY column_name ASC|DESC;
```

`column1, column2, ...`: These represent the columns you want to retrieve from your table.

`table_name`: This specifies the table containing the data you want to sort.

`column_name`: This defines the column you want to use for sorting.

`ASC`: This keyword sorts the data in ascending order (default if not specified).

`DESC`: This keyword sorts the data in descending order.

Example:

Let's say you want to retrieve all posts from your WordPress database, ordered by their post title alphabetically (A-Z). Here's the query:

```sql
SELECT post_title, post_content
```

FROM wp_posts

ORDER BY post_title ASC;

```

This query will retrieve the `post_title` and `post_content` columns from the `wp_posts` table and sort them alphabetically by the `post_title` in ascending order.

Sorting by Multiple Columns:

You can sort your data based on multiple columns by specifying them one after another in the `ORDER BY` clause. Here's an example:

```sql
SELECT post_title, post_date

FROM wp_posts

ORDER BY post_date DESC, post_title ASC;
```

This query will first sort the posts by their `post_date` in descending order (most recent first). Then, within posts with the same date, it will further sort by `post_title` in ascending order.

Sorting with NULL Values:
```

By default, NULL values are displayed at the end of the results when using `ORDER BY`. You can use the `NULLS FIRST` or `NULLS LAST` keywords to specify how NULL values should be handled:

`NULLS FIRST`: Places NULL values at the beginning of the sorted results.

`NULLS LAST`: Keeps NULL values at the end of the sorted results (default behavior).

Example:
```sql
SELECT user_name, user_email
FROM wp_users
ORDER BY user_email ASC NULLS LAST;
```

This query retrieves usernames and emails from the `wp_users` table, sorted by email addresses in ascending order. The `NULLS LAST` keyword ensures any users without email addresses appear at the end of the list.

The `ORDER BY` clause is applied after the data is retrieved from the database.

Sorting by multiple columns can be helpful for organizing complex data sets.

Understanding NULL value handling with `NULLS FIRST` and `NULLS LAST` helps you control how your results are displayed.

By mastering the `ORDER BY` clause, you can effectively organize your retrieved data from your WordPress database, making it easier to analyze and present information in a user-friendly manner.

Project: Write basic `SELECT` queries to retrieve specific data from your WordPress database.

Understanding `SELECT` Queries:

The `SELECT` statement is the foundation for retrieving data from a database table. It allows you to specify which data you want to extract and from which table. Here's the basic structure:

```sql
SELECT column1, column2, ...
FROM table_name
WHERE condition (optional);
```

`SELECT`: This keyword initiates the query, indicating you want to select data.

`column1, column2, ...`: This section lists the specific columns (fields) you want to retrieve from the table. You can select all columns with `` (asterisk).

`FROM`: This keyword specifies the table name from which you want to extract data.

`WHERE condition (optional)`: This clause allows you to filter the results based on specific criteria. We'll explore this later.

Steps to Write a Basic `SELECT` Query:

1. Log in to phpMyAdmin: Access your phpMyAdmin interface using the credentials provided by your web hosting service (refer to Chapter 2.1 for guidance).

2. Locate Your Database: In the left-hand panel, find your WordPress database (usually with a prefix like "wp_"). Click on it to expand and reveal the tables within.

Example: Retrieving All Posts

Let's write a query to retrieve all posts from your WordPress database:

1. Identify the Table: The posts in your WordPress website are stored in the `wp_posts` table.

2. Write the Query:

```sql
SELECT *
FROM wp_posts;
```

This query selects all columns (`*`) from the `wp_posts` table.

3. Execute the Query: In phpMyAdmin, locate the SQL query box at the bottom of the page. Paste your query into the box and click the "Go" button.

4. Results: phpMyAdmin will display the results in a table format, showing all the data stored in the `wp_posts` table. This includes information like post ID, title, content, author, and publication date.

Retrieving Specific Columns:

Instead of selecting all columns, you can specify the exact data points you're interested in:

```sql
SELECT post_title, post_content, post_date
FROM wp_posts;
```

This query retrieves only the `post_title`, `post_content`, and `post_date` columns from the `wp_posts` table.

Filtering Results with `WHERE` Clause:

The `WHERE` clause allows you to filter your results based on specific conditions. For example, let's retrieve all posts published after a certain date:

```sql
SELECT post_title, post_content, post_date
FROM wp_posts
WHERE post_date > '2024-03-20';  -- Replace '2024-03-20' with your desired date
```

This query retrieves posts where the `post_date` is greater than March 20th, 2024 (replace the date with your specific requirement).

Remember:

You can combine multiple conditions in the `WHERE` clause using logical operators like `AND` and `OR`.

Explore the phpMyAdmin documentation for detailed explanations of various filter options available in the `WHERE` clause.

By understanding the basic structure of `SELECT` queries and practicing with different examples, you've taken a significant step towards mastering MySQL queries for your WordPress website. As you progress through this book, you'll learn more advanced techniques for filtering, sorting, and manipulating data within your database, empowering you to unlock its full potential.

CHAPTER 4: WORKING WITH JOINS IN WORDPRESS

Learning Objectives: Understand and utilize joins to combine data from multiple tables for complex queries.

4.1 Demystifying Joins: Connecting Tables in Your Database

Imagine your WordPress website as a bustling city with various departments – the library holds books (posts), the town hall stores citizen information (users), and the marketplace keeps track of transactions (comments). While each department has its own data, there are often connections between them. For instance, a library book might be authored by a citizen, and a comment might be left on a specific post. This is where joins come in – they act like bridges, allowing you to combine data from multiple tables in your WordPress database for more complex queries.

Understanding Joins:

A join operation retrieves data from two or more tables based on a shared field (like a common ID). This enables you to fetch related data in a single query, improving efficiency and clarity. There are three main types of joins commonly used in WordPress:

INNER JOIN: Retrieves rows where there's a match in the joining field between both tables. Think of it as finding a specific citizen (user) who borrowed a particular book (post) from the library.

LEFT JOIN: Retrieves all rows from the left table (the "main" table) and matching rows from the right table. Even if there's no match in the right table, it will include those rows with null values for the joining field. Imagine finding all books (posts) in the library, even if some haven't been borrowed by any citizen (user) yet.

RIGHT JOIN: Similar to a LEFT JOIN, but it prioritizes the right table. It retrieves all rows from the right table and matching rows from the left table. This scenario could be useful if you want to find all users (with their information) who have ever borrowed a book (post), regardless of whether they have borrowed any books currently.

Example: INNER JOIN to Retrieve Posts and Authors

Let's look at a practical example of using an INNER JOIN to retrieve posts and their corresponding authors in WordPress. Here's a breakdown of the steps and code:

Identify Tables: We'll be working with two tables:

`wp_posts`: Stores information about blog posts, including the post ID (`ID`), title (`post_title`), and author ID (`post_author`).

`wp_users`: Contains user data, including the user ID (`ID`), username (`user_login`), and display name (`display_name`).

Write the Query: Here's the SQL code for the INNER JOIN query:

SQL

```
SELECT p.ID, p.post_title, u.display_name
FROM wp_posts AS p
INNER JOIN wp_users AS u ON p.post_author = u.ID;
```

Explanation of the Code:

`SELECT`: This keyword specifies the columns we want to retrieve from the tables.

`p.ID, p.post_title, u.display_name`: We're selecting the post ID (`ID`), post title (`post_title`), and user display name (`display_name`).

`FROM wp_posts AS p`: We specify the `wp_posts` table and alias it as `p` for easier reference.

`INNER JOIN wp_users AS u ON p.post_author = u.ID`: This is the join clause. It joins the `wp_posts` table (aliased as `p`) with the `wp_users` table (aliased as `u`) based on the condition `p.post_author = u.ID`. This essentially matches the post author ID (`post_author` in `wp_posts`) with the user ID (`ID` in `wp_users`).

`;`: This semicolon marks the end of the SQL query.

Executing the Query: This code can be executed directly in phpMyAdmin's query window or through a WordPress plugin that allows custom SQL queries.

Results: Running this query will return a list of posts along with their corresponding author's display name. This allows you to see which author wrote each post in a single result set.

Remember:

Joins can become more complex when dealing with multiple tables and conditions. However, understanding the basic concept of INNER JOIN, LEFT JOIN, and RIGHT JOIN is a foundation for crafting powerful queries to retrieve related data from your WordPress database.

Always ensure you're joining tables on appropriate and relevant fields to get accurate results.

4.2 Different Types of Joins: `INNER JOIN`, `LEFT JOIN`, and More

Imagine you're running a bustling online store built with WordPress. Your product information is stored in one table, and your customer information is stored in another. To display a customer's order history with product details, you'll need to combine data from both tables. This is where joins come in! Joins are powerful tools in SQL that allow you to retrieve data from multiple tables based on a related field.

In this section, we'll explore the most common types of joins used with WordPress databases:

- Inner Join
- Left Join
- Right Join
- Full Join

1. INNER JOIN: Matching Records Only

An `INNER JOIN` retrieves data only where there's a matching record in both tables. It's the most basic and commonly used join type.

Example: Let's say you have two tables:

`wp_posts`: Stores information about your products (product ID, title, description, etc.).

`wp_postmeta`: Stores additional product details (meta key, meta value) linked to the product ID in `wp_posts`.

You want to display a list of all products with their corresponding titles. Here's the SQL query using an `INNER JOIN`:

SQL

```
SELECT    p.post_id,    p.post_title,    pm.meta_value    AS product_description
FROM wp_posts AS p
INNER JOIN wp_postmeta AS pm ON p.ID = pm.post_id    -- Join on matching post ID
WHERE pm.meta_key = 'description'    -- Filter for 'description' meta key
```

Explanation:

`SELECT`: This clause specifies the columns you want to retrieve.

`p.post_id`: Selects the product ID from the `wp_posts` table (aliased as `p`).

`p.post_title`: Selects the product title from the `wp_posts` table.

`pm.meta_value AS product_description`: Selects the meta value from the `wp_postmeta` table (aliased as `pm`) and renames it to "product_description" for clarity.

`FROM wp_posts AS p`: Specifies the `wp_posts` table as the main table (aliased as `p`).

`INNER JOIN wp_postmeta AS pm ON p.ID = pm.post_id`: This is the join clause. It combines data from both tables where the `post_id` in `wp_posts` matches the `post_id` in `wp_postmeta`.

`WHERE pm.meta_key = 'description'`: This clause filters the `wp_postmeta` table to only include rows where the `meta_key` is "description" (assuming this stores your product descriptions).

This query will only return product data where there's a corresponding "description" entry in the `wp_postmeta` table. In simpler terms, it will only display products that have descriptions.

2. LEFT JOIN: Including All Records from the Left Table

A LEFT JOIN retrieves all records from the left table (the one specified first in the FROM clause) and matching records from the right table. If there's no match in the right table for a record in the left table, the corresponding columns from the right table will be filled with NULL values.

Example: Let's say you have a table named `wp_users` that stores user information and another table named `wp_orders` that stores order details with a `user_id` linking them. You want to display a list of all users, even those who haven't placed any orders yet.

SQL

SELECT u.ID AS user_id, u.user_login AS username, o.order_id, o.order_date

FROM wp_users AS u

LEFT JOIN wp_orders AS o ON u.ID = o.user_id -- Join on matching user ID

ORDER BY user_id ASC; -- Sort by user ID

Explanation:

This query is similar to the `INNER JOIN` example, but it uses `LEFT JOIN` instead.

The query will return all users from `wp_users` (left table) even if they don't have any orders in `wp_orders` (right table).

For users without orders, the `order_id` and `order_date` columns from `wp_orders` will be filled with NULL values.

The `ORDER BY`

4.3 Using Joins to Retrieve Related Data in WordPress (e.g., Posts and Comments)

Imagine your WordPress website as a bustling city with various departments (tables) storing information. The "posts" table acts like the city's library, holding articles and blog entries. The "comments" table, like the library's feedback cards, stores comments left on those posts. But how do you find out which comments belong to which posts? This is where joins come in – they act like bridges connecting related data from different tables in your database.

Understanding Joins:

A join operation combines data from two or more tables based on a shared field. This allows you to retrieve related information in a single query, saving time and effort.

There are different types of joins, but here we'll focus on two commonly used joins in WordPress:

INNER JOIN: Retrieves only rows where there's a match in both tables based on the join condition.

LEFT JOIN: Retrieves all rows from the left table (usually the main table) and matching rows from the right table. If there's no match in the right table for a specific row in the left table, it will return NULL values for the right table's columns.

Retrieving Posts with Comments (INNER JOIN)

Let's say you want to display a list of posts on your website, along with the number of comments each post has received. Here's how to achieve this using an INNER JOIN:

SQL Code:

SQL

```
SELECT p.post_title, p.post_content, COUNT(c.comment_ID) AS comment_count
FROM wp_posts AS p
INNER JOIN wp_comments AS c ON p.ID = c.comment_post_ID
GROUP BY p.ID;
```

SELECT: This clause specifies the columns you want to retrieve from the tables.

`p.post_title`: Retrieves the title of the post from the `wp_posts` table (aliased as `p`).

`p.post_content`: Retrieves the content of the post.

`COUNT(c.comment_ID) AS comment_count`: Counts the number of comments for each post using the `comment_ID` from the `wp_comments` table (aliased as `c`). The result is stored with the alias `comment_count`.

FROM: This clause specifies the tables involved in the join.

`wp_posts AS p`: The `wp_posts` table is aliased as `p` for easier reference.

`INNER JOIN wp_comments AS c`: We perform an INNER JOIN with the `wp_comments` table aliased as `c`.

ON: This clause defines the condition for joining the tables.

`p.ID = c.comment_post_ID`: We join the tables based on the `ID` column from `wp_posts` (which uniquely identifies each post) and the `comment_post_ID` column from `wp_comments` (which stores the ID of the post the comment belongs to).

GROUP BY: This clause groups the results by the `ID` of the post, ensuring we get the comment count for each unique post.

Running the Query:

You can execute this query directly in phpMyAdmin or use a plugin like "WP-DBManager" to run it within your WordPress dashboard.

Expected Output:

The query will return a list of your posts with their titles, content, and the corresponding number of comments for each post.

LEFT JOIN Example (Displaying All Posts with or Without Comments)

An INNER JOIN only returns rows with a matching record in both tables. What if you want to display all posts, even those without comments? Here's how a LEFT JOIN helps:

SQL

```
SELECT            p.post_title,           p.post_content,
COALESCE(COUNT(c.comment_ID), 0) AS comment_count
FROM wp_posts AS p
LEFT JOIN wp_comments AS c ON p.ID = c.comment_post_ID
GROUP BY p.ID;
```

This code is similar to the INNER JOIN example, but we use a LEFT JOIN instead. The `COALESCE` function ensures that even if there are no comments for a post (`COUNT(c.comment_ID)` returns NULL), the `comment_count` will display 0 instead.

Project: Practice writing queries using joins to retrieve data from multiple WordPress tables.

Alright, it's time to put your newfound knowledge of phpMyAdmin and MySQL queries to work! This project focuses on using joins, a powerful technique for combining data from multiple tables in your WordPress database.

Why Joins?

Imagine you have separate tables for storing blog posts (titles, content) and authors (names, bios). To display author information alongside each post on your website, you'd need to retrieve data from both tables. This is where joins come in. They allow you to connect related data across tables based on a common field, creating a unified result set.

The Scenario:

Let's create a simple scenario to practice joins. We'll retrieve a list of all blog posts from the `wp_posts` table, along with the author's name for each post. Here's what we need:

Access phpMyAdmin: Log in to your phpMyAdmin interface using the credentials provided by your web hosting service (refer to Chapter 2.1 for guidance).

Identify the Tables: We'll be working with two tables:

`wp_posts`: This table stores information about posts, including the post ID (`ID`), title (`post_title`), and author ID (`post_author`).

`wp_users`: This table stores user data, including the user ID (`ID`), username (`user_login`), and display name (`display_name`).

The Join Operation:

We'll use an `INNER JOIN` to connect the `wp_posts` and `wp_users` tables based on the `post_author` field in `wp_posts`. This field holds the user ID of the post author. Here's the SQL query we'll use:

SQL
```
SELECT p.ID, p.post_title, u.display_name
FROM wp_posts AS p
```

```
INNER JOIN wp_users AS u ON p.post_author = u.ID
ORDER BY p.ID DESC;
```

Breaking Down the Code:

`SELECT`: This keyword specifies the columns we want to retrieve from the tables.

`p.ID, p.post_title, u.display_name`: We're selecting the `ID`, `post_title` from `wp_posts` (aliased as `p`) and the `display_name` from `wp_users` (aliased as `u`).

`FROM wp_posts AS p`: This specifies the main table (`wp_posts`) and assigns it an alias `p` for easier reference.

`INNER JOIN wp_users AS u ON p.post_author = u.ID`: This is the crucial join part. We're joining the `wp_posts` table (aliased as `p`) with the `wp_users` table (aliased as `u`) based on the condition `p.post_author = u.ID`. This means the `post_author` ID in `wp_posts` must match the user ID (`ID`) in `wp_users` for a record to be included in the result set.

`ORDER BY p.ID DESC`: This clause sorts the results by post ID in descending order (most recent posts first).

Executing the Query:

Navigate to the SQL Tab: In phpMyAdmin, select your WordPress database and then click on the "SQL" tab at the top.

Paste the Query: Paste the code snippet mentioned above into the query editor box.

Run the Query: Click the "Go" button at the bottom of the page.

Understanding the Results:

If everything is set up correctly, phpMyAdmin will display a table with your query results. You should see a list of posts with their corresponding titles and author display names. This demonstrates how joins effectively combine data from multiple tables, providing a more comprehensive view of your website's content and authors.

CHAPTER 5: OPTIMIZING QUERIES FOR FASTER PERFORMANCE

Learning Objectives: Learn techniques to write efficient MySQL queries for a speedy website.

5.1 Understanding Query Performance: Identifying Slow Queries

Just like a car running low on fuel, your WordPress website can slow down if queries take too long to retrieve data from the database. These sluggish queries can lead to frustrating loading times for your visitors and a negative impact on your website's search engine ranking.

In this section, we'll delve into understanding query performance and how to identify slow queries that might be hindering your website's speed.

What is Query Performance?

Query performance refers to how fast your database retrieves data in response to a query. Think of a query as a specific question you ask your database, like "find all blog posts published in the last month." The faster the database can find and deliver the requested information, the better the query performance.

Why is Query Performance Important?

Slow queries can significantly impact your WordPress website in two ways:

User Experience: If queries take too long to execute, your website will take longer to load pages. This can lead to impatient visitors bouncing off your site before they even see your content.

Search Engine Optimization (SEO): Search engines like Google consider website speed a ranking factor. Slow loading times caused by sluggish queries can negatively affect your website's position in search results.

Identifying Slow Queries

Here are some ways to identify slow queries in your WordPress environment:

Using phpMyAdmin's Slow Query Log:

phpMyAdmin, the web interface for managing your MySQL database, offers a built-in feature called the "Slow Query Log." This log keeps track of queries that take longer than a certain threshold (which you can define) to execute.

To enable the Slow Query Log, access phpMyAdmin and navigate to your WordPress database. Look for the "Slow Query" section and follow the instructions to activate logging and set the desired time threshold.

Once enabled, the Slow Query Log will record information about slow queries, including the query itself, its execution time, and the time it took to return results. By analyzing this log, you can identify queries that are causing performance bottlenecks.

WordPress Performance Plugins:

Several WordPress plugins are designed to help you monitor website performance and identify slow queries. These plugins often provide user-friendly dashboards that display query execution times and other performance metrics.

Popular options include:

WP Rocket

WP Super Cache

Query Monitor

Here's an example of a simple code snippet you might see in a Slow Query Log:

```
# Time: 14:56:12
# User@Host: root@localhost
# Slow query: SELECT * FROM wp_posts WHERE post_type = 'post' AND post_status = 'publish' ORDER BY post_date DESC LIMIT 10;
# Lock time: 0.000000 sec
```

```
# Rows sent: 10   Rows examined: 1456
# Time: 0.340000 sec
```

Explanation of the Code Snippet:

This log entry shows a query that took 0.34 seconds to execute.

The query selects all posts (`*`) from the `wp_posts` table where the post type is `"post"` and the post status is `"publish"`.

The results are ordered by post date in descending order (`ORDER BY post_date DESC`) and limited to the 10 most recent posts (`LIMIT 10`).

While 0.34 seconds might seem like a small amount of time, if this query runs on every page load to retrieve recent posts, it can accumulate and slow down your website.

By identifying slow queries and optimizing them (covered in later chapters), you can significantly improve your website's performance and user experience.

5.2 Indexing Strategies: Supercharge Your Database Searches

Imagine a vast library – searching for a specific book can be time-consuming if you have to sift through every single one on the shelves. Thankfully, libraries use indexes – alphabetized catalogs –

to quickly locate the books you need. Similarly, indexes play a crucial role in optimizing database queries within your WordPress website.

Understanding Indexes:

An index is a special data structure within a database that acts like a catalog for specific columns (fields) in a table. It allows the database to quickly locate rows containing specific values in those columns.

Benefits of Indexing:

- **Faster Query Execution:** When a query searches for data based on an indexed column, the database can efficiently locate relevant rows using the index, significantly improving query performance.
- **Improved Website Speed:** Faster queries translate to faster loading times for your WordPress website, enhancing user experience and potentially boosting search engine ranking.

Types of Indexes:
- **Primary Key:** Every table should have a primary key, a unique identifier for each row. The database automatically creates an index on the primary key column for efficient data retrieval.
- **Secondary Indexes:** You can create additional indexes on specific columns that are frequently used in WHERE clause conditions within your queries.

Creating Indexes in phpMyAdmin:

1. **Log in to phpMyAdmin:** Access phpMyAdmin using your web hosting credentials (refer to Chapter 2.1 for guidance).
2. **Select Your Database:** In the left-hand panel, locate your WordPress database and click on it to expand the list of tables.
3. **Choose a Table:** Click on the table you want to optimize by indexing.
4. **Access the Structure Tab:** Locate the "Structure" tab at the top of the phpMyAdmin interface. This displays the table structure, including a list of columns.
5. **Adding an Index:** Find the column(s) where you want to create an index. Locate the "Indexes" section (might be named "Keys" in some versions). Click the "Add index" button.
6. **Index Configuration:** A popup window will appear for configuring the index. You can choose a name for the index and select the column(s) to include. By default, the "PRIMARY" option should be unchecked as you're creating a secondary index.

7. **Save the Index:** Once you've selected the desired columns, click the "Go" button at the bottom of the window to create the index.

Example (Adding Index on `post_title` column):

Here's an example of adding an index on the `post_title` column in the `wp_posts` table:

1. Access your WordPress database in phpMyAdmin.
2. Click on the `wp_posts` table.
3. Go to the "Structure" tab.
4. Locate the `post_title` column.
5. Click the "Add index" button in the "Indexes" section.
6. In the popup window, choose a name for the index (e.g., "title_index") and ensure the checkbox next to `post_title` is selected.
7. Click "Go" to create the index.

Strategic Indexing: Don't over-index your tables. Adding indexes on every column can have diminishing returns and might even slow down some queries. Focus on columns frequently used in WHERE clause conditions.

Analyze Query Performance: Tools like phpMyAdmin's "Slow query log" can help identify queries that are taking too long to execute. Analyze these queries to determine which columns might benefit from indexing.

5.3 Writing Optimized Queries: Best Practices to Avoid Bottlenecks

Imagine your website as a busy highway. When users submit queries to your database, it's like sending out tollbooth collectors to retrieve specific information. Just like on a highway, inefficiencies in your queries can lead to bottlenecks and slow down your website's performance. This section will equip you with best practices for writing optimized MySQL queries to ensure your website runs smoothly.

Understanding Query Optimization:

> **Query Optimization:** The process of structuring your queries to retrieve data from the database efficiently. Optimized queries minimize the time and resources required, resulting in faster website loading times.

Best Practices for Optimized Queries:

1. **Targeted Selection:**

Focus on retrieving only the data you need. Instead of using the wildcard (*) to select all columns from a table, explicitly list the specific columns you require in your `SELECT` statement. This reduces the amount of data transferred between the database and your website.

Example (Unoptimized):

SQL

```
SELECT * FROM wp_posts;
```
This query retrieves all columns from the `wp_posts` table, even if you only need a few specific pieces of information.

Example (Optimized):

SQL

```
SELECT post_id, post_title, post_content FROM wp_posts;
```
This optimized query retrieves only the `post_id`, `post_title`, and `post_content` columns, reducing data transfer and improving performance.

2. **Leveraging Indexes:**

Indexes are like alphabetized catalogs in a library. They help the database locate specific data quickly. When writing queries, consider which columns you frequently filter or sort by. Create indexes on those columns to significantly improve query performance.

Example:

If you frequently search for blog posts by title, creating an index on the `post_title` column can dramatically speed up those queries.

3. **WHERE Clause Efficiency:**

The `WHERE` clause filters your data based on specific conditions. Here are some tips for using it effectively:

- ➤ **Place it Early:** Position the `WHERE` clause towards the beginning of your query. This allows the database to filter data early on, reducing the amount of data it needs to process further.
- ➤ **Avoid Complex Conditions:** Break down complex conditions into simpler ones whenever possible. The database can evaluate simpler conditions more efficiently.
- ➤ **Use Appropriate Operators:** Utilize operators like `=`, `>`, `<`, and `LIKE` effectively. Avoid functions or calculations within the `WHERE` clause whenever possible, as they can slow down the filtering process.

Example (Unoptimized):

SQL

```
SELECT * FROM wp_posts WHERE post_title LIKE '%search term%';
```

This query uses the `LIKE` operator with a wildcard (`%`), which requires the database to scan through all titles.

Example (Optimized):

SQL

```
SELECT * FROM wp_posts WHERE post_title = 'exact search term';
```

This optimized query uses an exact comparison (`=`) which is much faster for the database to evaluate.

4. LIMIT Clause:

The `LIMIT` clause restricts the number of results returned by your query. This is particularly helpful for paginating large datasets or preventing overwhelming amounts of data from being retrieved.

Example:

SQL

```
SELECT * FROM wp_posts LIMIT 10;
```

This query retrieves only the first 10 results from the `wp_posts` table.

Additional Tips:

Use explain to analyze queries: phpMyAdmin offers an "EXPLAIN" feature that analyzes your query and displays its execution plan. This can help you identify potential bottlenecks and areas for further optimization.

Keep it Simple: Strive for clear and concise queries. Complex logic within your queries can be difficult to maintain and optimize in the long run.

Project: Analyze slow queries in your WordPress environment and optimize them for better performance.

Does your WordPress website feel sluggish? Slow loading times can frustrate visitors and negatively impact your search engine ranking. One culprit for sluggishness can be inefficient database queries. In this project, you'll learn how to identify slow queries in your WordPress environment and optimize them for better performance.

Understanding Slow Queries:

- **Query:** An instruction sent to the database to retrieve specific information.
- **Slow Query:** A query that takes an unusually long time to execute, causing delays in loading your website content.

There are several reasons why queries might become slow:

- **Inefficient code:** Queries written without best practices in mind can lead to unnecessary database processing time.
- **Complex data relationships:** Queries involving many tables or complex joins can take longer to execute.
- **Database Issues:** Underlying problems with the database itself (e.g., lack of indexing) can hinder query performance.

Identifying Slow Queries:

Here's how to identify slow queries in your WordPress environment:

1. **Access phpMyAdmin:** Log in to your phpMyAdmin interface using the credentials provided by your web hosting service (refer to Chapter 2.1 for guidance).
2. **Enable Slow Query Logging:** In phpMyAdmin, locate the "Slow query log" section. This option might be under the "Variables" or "Performance" tab depending on your web hosting configuration. You'll need to enable logging by setting the "slow_query_log" variable to "ON" and defining

a minimum query execution time (e.g., 1 second) in the "long_query_time" variable. Save the changes.
3. **Replicate Slow Website Actions:** Once logging is enabled, visit your WordPress website and perform actions that typically lead to slow loading times (e.g., browsing specific pages, searching for content). The slow query log will capture these inefficient queries.
4. **Reviewing the Slow Query Log:** After replicating slow website actions, return to phpMyAdmin and navigate to the "Slow query log" section (location might vary based on your web hosting setup). You'll see a list of logged queries, including details like:

- **Time:** Execution time of the query.
- **User:** The database user who ran the query (usually your WordPress installation).
- **Query:** The actual SQL code of the slow query.
- **Lock Time:** Time spent waiting for table locks (indicating potential bottlenecks).
- **Rows examined:** Number of rows scanned by the database to execute the query.

Optimizing Slow Queries:

Now that you've identified slow queries, let's explore some optimization techniques:

1. **Analyze the Query:** Carefully examine the slow query's SQL code. Look for areas for improvement, such as unnecessary filtering clauses, complex joins, or missing indexes.

2. **Simplify Code:** If the query involves excessive filtering or conditions, try to simplify it by using more concise WHERE clauses or eliminating unnecessary logic.
3. **Leverage Indexing:** Indexes are like reference guides for your database tables. Properly configured indexes can significantly speed up queries by allowing the database to locate specific data efficiently. You might need to research how to create or optimize indexes for your specific slow query using the identified tables.
4. **Utilize Caching Plugins:** Consider using caching plugins that store frequently accessed data, reducing the need for repetitive queries on your database. However, choose plugins with good reputations and be mindful of potential conflicts with other plugins.

Example Code Snippet (Illustrative Purposes Only):

Imagine a slow query retrieves all blog posts from the `wp_posts` table without any filtering. Here's the (inefficient) code:

SQL

```
SELECT * FROM wp_posts;
```

This query scans the entire `wp_posts` table, which can be slow for large datasets. An optimized version might involve filtering for recent posts only:

SQL

```
SELECT * FROM wp_posts WHERE post_date >
DATE_SUB(CURDATE(), INTERVAL 7 DAY);
```

This optimized query only retrieves posts from the past week, reducing the number of rows scanned and improving performance.

Optimizing queries often requires analyzing the specific code and understanding the underlying database structure. However, the techniques mentioned above provide a good starting point for tackling slow queries in your WordPress environment.

Testing and Monitoring:
Once you've optimized a slow query, it's crucial to test the results. Disable slow query logging temporarily and revisit your website to see if the loading times have improved. Additionally, consider using performance monitoring plugins that track database query times over time, allowing you to identify recurring slow queries and optimize them proactively.

CHAPTER 6: WORKING WITH USERS AND USER DATA

Learning Objectives: Master querying and managing user data within your WordPress database.

6.1 Exploring the `wp_users` Table: Understanding User Data Structure

6.1 Exploring the `wp_users` Table: Understanding User Data Structure

Users are the lifeblood of any website, and WordPress is no exception. The `wp_users` table stores all the essential information about the users registered on your WordPress site. Understanding its structure is crucial for managing user data and potentially creating custom queries to retrieve specific user information.

Locating the `wp_users` Table:

1. **Access phpMyAdmin:** Log in to your phpMyAdmin interface using the credentials provided by your web hosting service (refer to Chapter 2.1 for guidance).
2. **Identify Your Database:** In the left-hand panel, locate the database name containing your WordPress data (usually with a prefix like "wp_"). Click on it to expand the list of tables.
3. **Find `wp_users`:** Among the listed tables, you should see one named `wp_users`. Click on it to view its structure.

Understanding User Data Columns:

The `wp_users` table will display a list of columns, each representing a specific piece of user information. Here's a breakdown of some key columns:

- **ID (INT):** A unique identifier assigned to each user. This is the primary key of the table, meaning no two users can have the same ID.

- **user_login (VARCHAR(255)):** The username chosen by the user during registration. This is typically used for logging in to the website.

- **user_pass (VARCHAR(255)):** Stores the user's password. However, it's crucial to understand that passwords are never stored in plain text within the database. WordPress uses a one-way hashing algorithm to encrypt passwords for security purposes. You won't be able to see the actual password itself.

- **user_email (VARCHAR(255)):** The user's email address used for registration and communication.

- **user_nicename (VARCHAR(255)):** A unique, URL-friendly version of the username, often used for creating user profile URLs.

- **user_url (VARCHAR(255)):** The user's website URL, if provided during registration.

- **user_registered (DATETIME):** Date and time the user registered on your website.

Additional Columns

Depending on your WordPress configuration and installed plugins, the `wp_users` table might contain additional columns for storing user-specific data. These might include:

- **user_activation_key (VARCHAR(255)):** Used for activating user accounts after registration (if enabled).

- **user_meta (LONGTEXT):** Stores serialized user meta data added by plugins or themes.

Exploring User Data:

Clicking on a specific column name in the table structure view allows you to browse actual user data entries within that column. You'll see a list of usernames, email addresses, or other information depending on the chosen column.

Remember:

- **Security:** The `user_pass` column stores hashed passwords, not the actual passwords themselves. Never attempt to modify this data directly.
- **User Management:** While phpMyAdmin allows basic editing of user data, it's generally recommended to

manage users through the WordPress administration panel for better control and security.

6.2 Retrieving Specific User Information with Targeted Queries

Your WordPress website thrives on its users. Understanding who your users are and what information they provide allows you to personalize content, manage user roles, and maintain a healthy online community. This section dives into crafting targeted MySQL queries using phpMyAdmin to retrieve specific user information from your WordPress database.

Understanding the `wp_users` Table:
WordPress stores user information in a dedicated table named `wp_users`. This table holds various data points about your users, including:

- `ID` (Primary Key): A unique identifier assigned to each user.
- `user_login`: The username used for logging in.
- `user_email`: The user's email address.
- `user_nicename`: A user-friendly version of the username for URLs.
- `user_registered`: The date and time the user registered on your website. (Stored in a timestamp format)

- **Many More:** The `wp_users` table contains additional fields depending on your WordPress plugins and settings.

Crafting Your Query:

To retrieve specific user information, we'll leverage the power of the `SELECT` statement in MySQL. Here's a general structure:

SQL

```
SELECT desired_columns
FROM wp_users
WHERE specific_condition;
```

Explanation:
- `SELECT desired_columns`: This specifies the exact columns (data points) you want to retrieve from the `wp_users` table. You can select a single column (e.g., `user_email`) or multiple columns separated by commas (e.g., `user_login, user_email`).
- `FROM wp_users`: This defines the table you're querying data from, which is the `wp_users` table in this case.
- `WHERE specific_condition`: This optional clause allows you to filter your results based on specific criteria. We'll explore different filtering conditions in the following examples.

Example 1: Retrieving All Users

To retrieve information for all registered users on your website, you can use the following query:

SQL
```
SELECT *
FROM wp_users;
```

Explanation:
- `*` in the `SELECT` clause acts as a wildcard, indicating you want to retrieve all columns (data points) from the `wp_users` table.
- This query will return a list of all users with their corresponding information in the table.

Example 2: Retrieving a Specific User by ID

If you know a user's unique ID, you can retrieve their information using the following query:

SQL
```
SELECT *
FROM wp_users
WHERE ID = specific_user_id;
```

Explanation:
- The `WHERE` clause filters the results based on the `ID` column.

- Replace `specific_user_id` with the actual user ID you want to retrieve information for. This ID can be found by exploring the `wp_users` table in phpMyAdmin or by using other WordPress functionalities to identify user IDs.

Example 3: Retrieving Users by Email Address

To find users based on their email address, use the following query:

SQL
```
SELECT *
FROM wp_users
WHERE user_email = 'user_email@example.com';
```

Explanation:

- We replaced `specific_user_id` with `user_email` to filter by the `user_email` column.
- Enclose the email address in single quotes. Replace `user_email@example.com` with the actual email address you want to search for.

Additional Filtering Options:

The WHERE clause offers various comparison operators for filtering your results. Here are some common examples:
- `=` (Equal to): Used in the previous examples.
- `!=` (Not equal to): Find users with email addresses different from a specific address.

- `LIKE`: Perform pattern matching for partial matches (e.g., `user_login LIKE '%admin%'` would retrieve usernames containing "admin").
- ➤ (Greater than): Find users who registered after a specific date (requires timestamp manipulation).
- `<` (Less than): Find users who registered before a specific date (requires timestamp manipulation).

Running Your Query in phpMyAdmin:
1. Log in to phpMyAdmin using your web hosting credentials.
2. Select your WordPress database from the left-hand panel.
3. Click on the "SQL" tab at the top of the interface.
4. Paste your desired query (e.g., any of the examples above) into the query window.
5. Click the "Go" button at the bottom of the page.

phpMyAdmin will execute your query and display the results in a table format. You can then analyze the retrieved information or

6.3 Managing Users and User Roles through Database Actions

Important Note: While this section explores managing users and user roles through the database, it's crucial to understand that modifying the database directly should be a last resort. The WordPress administration panel offers a user-friendly interface for these tasks, minimizing the risk of errors. **Proceed with caution** if you choose to manage users via the database, and **always back up your database before making any changes.**

This section is intended for users comfortable with SQL queries and understand the potential risks involved.

Understanding User Management in WordPress:
WordPress utilizes a user roles system to define the permissions users have on your website. Here's a breakdown of some common user roles:

- **Administrator:** Has full control over the website, including adding/editing users, managing posts, and installing plugins.
- **Editor:** Can create, edit, and publish posts, but cannot manage other users or themes.
- **Author:** Can write and edit their own posts, but cannot publish them (requires review by an Editor or Administrator).
- **Contributor:** Can create new posts but cannot publish them or edit existing ones.
- **Subscriber:** Can only manage their profile information.

User Data Structure:

The `wp_users` table in your WordPress database stores user information. Here's a simplified breakdown of some key columns:

- **ID (INT):** Unique identifier for each user.
- **user_login (VARCHAR):** Username used for logging in.
- **user_email (VARCHAR):** User's email address.
- **user_pass (VARCHAR):** Hashed password (**never store plain text passwords!**).

- **user_registered (DATETIME):** Date and time the user registered.
- **user_role (VARCHAR):** User's assigned role (e.g., "administrator," "editor").

Modifying User Roles with SQL Queries:

Example 1: Changing a User's Role from Contributor to Editor

1. **Access phpMyAdmin:** Log in to your phpMyAdmin interface as described in Chapter 2.1.
2. **Select the `wp_users` Table:** In the left-hand panel, locate your WordPress database and click on the `wp_users` table.
3. **Edit User Row:** Locate the user you want to modify. You can identify them by their username or email address in the `user_login` or `user_email` column. Click the "Edit" link next to the desired user.

Important: You'll see a large text field containing various user data. Be very careful when editing this data directly.

4. **Update the `user_role` Value:** In the text field, locate the line containing `user_role` (usually towards the bottom). Change the value after the colon (:) from "contributor" to "editor".

Code Snippet (for reference only, editing directly in phpMyAdmin is recommended):

SQL

```sql
UPDATE wp_users
SET user_role = 'editor'
WHERE ID = [user_id];

**Replace [user_id] with the actual user ID number from
your table.**
```

5. **Save Changes:** Click the "Go" button at the bottom of the page to save your modifications.

Example 2: Adding a New User with a Specific Role

Caution: This example requires inserting a new row into the database, which can be more complex and error-prone. It's generally recommended to use the WordPress user registration functionality for adding new users.

6. **Access the `wp_users` Table:** Follow steps 1 and 2 from Example 1.
7. **Insert New Row:** Click the "Insert" tab at the top of the phpMyAdmin interface.
8. **Fill in User Data:** In the corresponding fields, enter the new user's information like username, email address, and desired password (remember to use a secure password hashing function before inserting).
9. **Set User Role:** In the `user_role` field, specify the desired role (e.g., "author").

Code Snippet (for reference only, not recommended for beginners):
SQL

```sql
INSERT INTO wp_users (user_login, user_email, user_pass,
user_registered, user_role)
```

```
VALUES ('[username]', '[email]', '[hashed_password]',
NOW(), '[user_role]');
```

Replace the bracketed values with the actual user information and hashed password.

5. **Save Changes:** Click the "Go" button at the bottom of the page to create the new user with the assigned role.

Remember:
- Modifying the database directly carries inherent risks. Always back up your database

Project: Write queries to retrieve specific user information and practice basic user management through the database *(if applicable to your skill level)*.

This project will guide you through writing queries in phpMyAdmin to retrieve specific user information and practice basic user management tasks within your WordPress database. **Important Note:** While this project demonstrates these functionalities, modifying user data directly through the database is generally not recommended for everyday WordPress management. It's safer to use the built-in WordPress user administration tools. However, understanding these queries can be valuable for troubleshooting or specific scenarios.

Prerequisites:
- ❖ Access to your WordPress database through phpMyAdmin (refer to Chapter 2.1 for login instructions).

❖ Basic understanding of SQL syntax (SELECT, WHERE, UPDATE, etc.).

Steps:
1. **Log in to phpMyAdmin:** Use your web hosting credentials to access phpMyAdmin.
2. **Select Your Database:** In the left-hand panel, locate your WordPress database (usually with a prefix like "wp_"). Click on it to expand and reveal the tables.
3. **Retrieving User Information:**

We'll use the `wp_users` table to retrieve user information. This table stores data about all registered users on your WordPress site.

Task 1: Get All Users

- Locate the `SELECT` tab at the top of the phpMyAdmin interface.
- In the main text area, write the following query:

SQL

```sql
SELECT * FROM wp_users;
```

- Click the "Go" button at the bottom of the page.

This query retrieves all columns (indicated by "*") from the `wp_users` table. The results will display a list of users with their corresponding data, including username, email address (hashed for security), user ID, and other user-related information.

Task 2: Get User by Username

- Let's modify the query to retrieve information for a specific user based on their username.

SQL

```
SELECT * FROM wp_users WHERE user_login = 'your_username_here';
```

- Replace `'your_username_here'` with the actual username of the user you want to retrieve information for.
- Click "Go" to execute the query.

This query uses the `WHERE` clause to filter results based on the `user_login` column (which stores usernames). It will return information only for the user with the matching username.

4. Basic User Management (Use with Caution):

Disclaimer: While this section demonstrates basic user management through queries, it's generally recommended to use the WordPress user administration panel for managing users. Modifying user data directly in the database can have unintended consequences and should be done with caution.

Task 3: Update User Email (Use with Caution):

- Here's a sample query to update a user's email address:

SQL

```
UPDATE wp_users SET user_email = 'new_email@example.com' WHERE user_login = 'your_username_here';
```

- Replace `'new_email@example.com'` with the new email address you want to assign. Ensure it's a valid email address.

- Replace `'your_username_here'` with the username of the user whose email you want to update.
- Click "Go" to execute the query. **Important:** This will permanently update the user's email address in the database.

Remember: Modifying user data directly through the database should be a last resort. It's safer and more user-friendly to use the built-in WordPress user administration tools for most user management tasks.

5. Conclusion:

This project provided a hands-on introduction to writing basic MySQL queries to retrieve user information and (with caution) perform basic user management tasks within your WordPress database. Remember, the WordPress user administration panel offers a safer and more controlled environment for managing users on your website. However, understanding these queries can be beneficial for troubleshooting purposes or specific scenarios.

Additional Notes:
- This project focused on basic functionalities. phpMyAdmin offers various options for managing database tables, including deleting entries. However, exercise extreme caution when deleting user data from the database, as it's not reversible.

- Security is paramount. Ensure you have a recent backup of your database before making any modifications through queries.

CHAPTER 7: CUSTOM POST TYPES AND DATA MANAGEMENT

Learning Objectives: Learn to query and manage custom post type data in your WordPress database.

7.1 Unveiling Custom Post Type Tables: Structure and Data Storage

WordPress offers a powerful feature called "Custom Post Types" that allows you to extend its functionality beyond the basic posts and pages. When you create a custom post type (e.g., Products, Events, Portfolio Items), WordPress creates a dedicated table in your database to store all the data associated with that type of content.

Understanding Custom Post Type Tables:

Imagine a filing cabinet with labeled folders. Each folder (custom post type) holds specific documents (posts) containing relevant information. These documents have sections (custom fields) to store details like titles, descriptions, and additional data unique to that post type.

- **Custom Post Type Table:** A dedicated table in your database that stores all the data for a specific custom post type. This table has a similar structure to the default WordPress tables (like `wp_posts`) but with

additional columns to accommodate the custom fields associated with that post type.
- **Columns:** These represent the different data points stored for each post within the custom post type. Default columns might include the post ID, title, content, and publication date. Additional columns are created for custom fields defined for that specific post type.
- **Rows:** Each row in the table represents a single post belonging to the custom post type. The data in each row corresponds to the specific post (e.g., title, content, custom field values).

Exploring the Structure:

While the exact structure of your custom post type table can vary depending on the specific fields you define, here's a general breakdown:

- **Core Columns:** These columns exist in most WordPress tables and store essential information about the post itself. They might include:
    - `ID`: A unique identifier for each post.
    - `post_title`: The title of the post.
    - `post_content`: The main content of the post.
    - `post_date`: The date and time the post was published.

- - `post_status`: The current status of the post (e.g., draft, published).
- **Custom Field Columns:** These columns are dynamically added based on the custom fields you define for your custom post type. Each custom field gets its own column to store the corresponding data for each post.
  - Example: If you create a custom field named "product_price" for a "Products" custom post type, a new column named "product_price" will be added to the table to store the price of each product.

Benefits of Understanding Structure:

By understanding how custom post type tables are structured, you gain several advantages:

- **Writing Targeted Queries:** You can write more precise queries to retrieve specific data from your custom post types. Knowing the column names allows you to target the exact information you need.
- **Data Manipulation:** If comfortable with SQL, you can potentially manipulate data within the custom post type table directly (though caution is advised and backups are crucial).

- **Troubleshooting Issues:** Understanding the table structure can aid in troubleshooting issues related to custom post types and their associated data.

7.2 Querying Custom Post Type Data with Tailored Statements

WordPress allows you to create custom post types to organize content beyond the default "posts" and "pages." These custom post types can have their own unique data fields, making it essential to know how to query and retrieve this specific information.

Understanding Custom Post Type Data:
- **Custom Post Types:** Think of them as specialized categories for your content, allowing you to create structures tailored to your specific needs (e.g., "Products" for an e-commerce store, "Recipes" for a food blog).
- **Custom Fields:** These are additional data points associated with your custom post types. For instance, a "Products" custom post type might have custom fields for "price," "stock," and "category."

Tailoring Queries for Custom Post Types:

The core structure of a MySQL query to retrieve data remains similar to what you learned for regular posts and pages. However, you'll need to adjust the table names and potentially add filters to target specific custom post types and their associated data.

Here's a simplified breakdown:
1. SELECT **Clause:** Specify the data fields you want to retrieve (e.g., "post_title," custom field names).
2. FROM **Clause:** Instead of using "wp_posts," you'll reference the table specific to your custom post type. This table name typically follows a format like "wp_{custom_post_type_name}" (e.g., "wp_products" for a "Products" custom post type).
3. WHERE **Clause (Optional):** You can add filters here to target specific entries within your custom post type. For example, you might filter by a custom field value or a specific category within your custom post type.

Example (Conceptual):

Imagine you have a custom post type named "Books" with custom fields for "author" and "genre." Here's a conceptual example of a query to retrieve all book titles and their corresponding authors:

SQL
```
SELECT post_title, author (custom field name)
FROM wp_books
```

Custom post types (CPTs) extend the functionality of WordPress by allowing you to create content types beyond standard posts and pages. Imagine a scenario where you have a custom post type for "Products" on your e-commerce website. Each product might have attributes like title, description, price, and category. This section will equip you with the skills to query and retrieve specific data from your custom post type tables using MySQL.

Understanding Custom Post Type Tables:

WordPress doesn't store custom post type data directly in the traditional "posts" table. Instead, it creates separate tables specifically for each custom post type. These tables typically follow a naming convention that starts with "wp_" followed by the custom post type name (singular form) and an underscore ("_"). For instance, a custom post type named "Products" would likely have a corresponding table named "wp_products".

Steps to Query Custom Post Type Data:
1. **Identify the Custom Post Type Table Name:**
    - Navigate to your WordPress dashboard.
    - Go to **WP Admin -> Posts -> All Custom Post Types**.
    - Locate your custom post type (e.g., Products). Hover over the name, and a small box will appear displaying the internal slug. This slug is often used to construct the custom post type table name (e.g., "wp_products").
2. **Connect to phpMyAdmin:**

- Use the login credentials provided by your web hosting service to access phpMyAdmin (refer to Chapter 2.1 for guidance).

3. **Write Your MySQL Query:**
    - In phpMyAdmin, select the database containing your WordPress data.
    - Now you can craft your query to retrieve data from the custom post type table. Here's a basic example:

SQL

```
SELECT * FROM wp_products;
```

This query selects all columns (*) from the `wp_products` table.

4. **Execute the Query:**
    - Once you've written your query, click the "Go" button at the bottom of the phpMyAdmin interface. The results will be displayed in a table format, showing all data points (rows) and columns from the custom post type table.

Extracting Specific Data:

The above example retrieved all data from the custom post type table. To target specific information, you can modify your query using the `SELECT` clause and specify the desired columns:

SQL

```
SELECT post_title, post_content, product_price FROM wp_products;
```

This query retrieves only three specific columns: `post_title`, `post_content`, and `product_price` (assuming these are column names in your custom post type table).

Filtering Results with WHERE Clause:

You can further refine your queries using the WHERE clause to filter results based on specific criteria. For example, to retrieve products with a price greater than $100:

SQL

```sql
SELECT * FROM wp_products WHERE product_price > 100;
```

This query selects all columns (*) from `wp_products` where the `product_price` is greater than 100.

- Replace `wp_products` with the actual table name for your custom post type.
- Adjust the column names (`post_title`, `post_content`, `product_price`) to match your specific custom post type schema.
- Experiment with different SELECT and WHERE clauses to target the exact data you need from your custom post type.

7.3 Filtering and Sorting Custom Post Types for Specific Needs

Custom post types (CPTs) extend the functionality of WordPress by allowing you to create content types beyond the default posts and pages. Imagine a website showcasing different recipes. You could create a custom post type called "Recipe" with specific fields for ingredients, cooking instructions, and difficulty level. But what if you want to display only vegetarian recipes or sort them by cooking time? This is where filtering and sorting queries come in!

Understanding Filtering and Sorting:

- **Filtering:** This process allows you to narrow down the results of your custom post type query based on specific criteria. Think of it like sifting through flour to find only the brown sugar for your recipe.
- **Sorting:** This process arranges the retrieved custom post type data in a particular order. Imagine organizing your spice rack alphabetically for easy access.

Filtering Custom Post Types with WHERE Clause:

The WHERE clause is a powerful tool for filtering your CPT queries. Here's a breakdown of the steps and code:

1. **Basic CPT Query:** Let's assume you have a custom post type named "Recipe" with a custom field called "Diet" (e.g., "Vegan," "Vegetarian," "Omnivore"). Here's a basic query that retrieves all recipes:

SQL

```
SELECT * FROM wp_posts p
INNER JOIN wp_postmeta pm ON p.ID = pm.post_id
WHERE p.post_type = 'recipe'
```

This code retrieves all posts (`*`) from the `wp_posts` table (`p`) and joins them with the `wp_postmeta` table (`pm`) to access custom field data. The `WHERE` clause filters for posts where the `post_type` is "recipe."

2. **Filtering by Custom Field:** Now, let's modify the query to show only vegetarian recipes:

SQL

```
SELECT * FROM wp_posts p
INNER JOIN wp_postmeta pm ON p.ID = pm.post_id
WHERE p.post_type = 'recipe'
AND pm.meta_key = 'Diet'    -- Target the custom field "Diet"
AND pm.meta_value = 'Vegetarian'    -- Filter for recipes with "Diet" value of "Vegetarian"
```

We've added an additional condition to the `WHERE` clause. We check if the `meta_key` (name of the custom field) is "Diet" and the `meta_value` (data stored in the field) is "Vegetarian." This filters the results to show only recipes with the "Diet" set to "Vegetarian."

Sorting Custom Post Types with ORDER BY Clause:

Once you have filtered your results, you can organize them using the ORDER BY clause. Here's an example:

SQL

```sql
SELECT * FROM wp_posts p
INNER JOIN wp_postmeta pm ON p.ID = pm.post_id
WHERE p.post_type = 'recipe'
AND pm.meta_key = 'Diet'
AND pm.meta_value = 'Vegetarian'
ORDER BY pm.meta_value ASC   -- Sort by "Diet" value in ascending order (A-Z)
```

Here, we've added the `ORDER BY` clause with `pm.meta_value ASC`. This sorts the retrieved recipes in ascending order based on the value stored in the "Diet" custom field (A-Z). You can also use `DESC` for descending order (Z-A).

Replace "recipe" and "Diet" with the actual names of your custom post type and custom field.

You can filter and sort based on multiple custom fields by adding additional conditions to the `WHERE` clause.

Additional Considerations:

- **Date Sorting:** You can sort by the post publish date using `p.post_date ASC` or `DESC`.
- **Complex Queries:** For more intricate filtering and sorting scenarios, consider using conditional statements and operators within your `WHERE` clause.

7.4 Creating a Custom Loop to Display Filtered and Sorted Recipes

Now that you can filter and sort your custom post type queries, let's put that knowledge into action! We'll create a basic WordPress template using a loop to display only vegetarian recipes sorted by cooking time (ascending order).

Here's a breakdown of the steps and code:
1. **Template File:** Create a new template file (e.g., `custom-recipes.php`) and place it within your theme's directory.
2. **Start the Loop:** Within your template file, use the standard WordPress loop construct to iterate through the filtered and sorted recipes. Here's the basic structure:

PHP

```php
<?php
  $args = array(
    'post_type' => 'recipe',     // Specify your custom post type
    'meta_key' => 'Diet',        // Target the custom field "Diet"
    'meta_value' => 'Vegetarian', // Filter for vegetarian recipes
    'orderby' => 'meta_value_num', // Sort by numeric value of "Diet" custom field
    'order' => 'ASC'             // Sort in ascending order (cooking time)
  );

  $query = new WP_Query( $args );

  if ( $query->have_posts() ) {
    while ( $query->have_posts() ) {
      $query->the_post();
      // Display recipe details here (refer to point 3)
    }
  } else {
    echo 'No vegetarian recipes found!';
  }

  wp_reset_postdata();
?>
```

Explanation:
- We define an array called `$args` containing arguments for the `WP_Query` object.
- We specify the `post_type` as "recipe" and filter for recipes with the "Diet" field value set to "Vegetarian."
- We use `orderby` set to `meta_value_num` to sort by the numeric value stored in the "Diet" custom field (assuming cooking time is stored as a number).
- The `order` is set to `ASC` for ascending order (shortest cooking time first).
- We create a new `WP_Query` object using the `$args` array to execute the customized query.
- The loop iterates through each retrieved recipe using `while ( $query->have_posts() )`.
- Inside the loop, we call `the_post()` to make the current post data available within the loop.

3. **Displaying Recipe Details:**

Within the loop, you can utilize standard WordPress functions to display the recipe details you want. Here's an example:

PHP

```php
    echo '<h2><a href="' . get_the_permalink() . '">' . get_the_title() . '</a></h2>';
    echo '<p>Cooking Time: ' . get_post_meta( get_the_ID(), 'Cooking_Time', true ) . ' minutes</p>';
    echo '<div>' . get_the_content() . '</div>';
```

This code snippet displays the recipe title (linked to the post), cooking time retrieved from a custom field named "Cooking_Time," and the post content. You can customize this section to showcase any recipe information you desire.

4. **Reset Post Data:** After the loop, call `wp_reset_postdata()` to reset global post data to avoid conflicts with other template parts.

- Modify the code to reflect your specific custom post type name, custom field names, and desired display elements.
- This is a basic example. You can enhance the template by adding styling, images, and additional functionalities.

Project: Write queries to retrieve and manipulate data from custom post types in your WordPress site.

This project will guide you through writing practical MySQL queries to retrieve and manipulate data from custom post types (CPTs) in your WordPress website.

Imagine you have a custom post type called "Product" with various custom fields to store product information like name, price, category, and stock availability. You want to achieve the following tasks using MySQL queries:

1. Retrieve All Products:

This query displays a list of all products with their titles (post titles) and IDs.

Steps:
1. **Access phpMyAdmin:** Log in to your phpMyAdmin interface using the credentials provided by your web hosting service (refer to Chapter 2.1 for guidance).
2. **Write the Query:** In the SQL query editor, type the following code:

SQL
```
SELECT p.ID, p.post_title
FROM wp_posts p
WHERE p.post_type = 'product'
```

Explanation:
- `SELECT p.ID, p.post_title`: This line specifies the data we want to retrieve - the post ID (`p.ID`) and post title (`p.post_title`).
- `FROM wp_posts p`: This defines the table from which we'll retrieve data - the `wp_posts` table (`p`) is used as an alias for easier reference.

- `WHERE p.post_type = 'product'`: This filters the results to only include posts where the `post_type` is "product".
3. **Execute the Query:** Click the "Go" button at the bottom of the page to execute the query. phpMyAdmin will display the results in a table format, showing the product IDs and corresponding titles.

2. Filter Products by Category:

Let's say you have a custom field named "product_category" to categorize your products. This query retrieves all products belonging to the "Electronics" category.

Steps:

1. **Modify the Query:** Update the previous code with the following changes:

SQL

```sql
SELECT p.ID, p.post_title
FROM wp_posts p
INNER JOIN wp_postmeta pm ON p.ID = pm.post_id
WHERE p.post_type = 'product'
AND pm.meta_key = 'product_category'
AND pm.meta_value = 'Electronics'
```

Explanation:

- We've introduced an `INNER JOIN` statement. This joins the `wp_posts` table (p) with the `wp_postmeta` table (pm) based on the post ID (`p.ID = pm.post_id`). This allows us to access custom field data stored in `wp_postmeta`.
- The additional `WHERE` clause conditions filter for products where the `meta_key` is "product_category" and the `meta_value` is "Electronics".

2. **Execute the Query:** Run the modified query. The results will only show products with the "Electronics" category.

3. Update Product Stock:

Suppose a specific product (ID: 123) has sold out, and you want to update its stock availability stored in a custom field named "stock_count" to 0.

Steps:

1. **Update Query:** Here's the code to update the stock:

SQL
```sql
UPDATE wp_postmeta
SET meta_value = 0
WHERE post_id = 123
AND meta_key = 'stock_count'
```

Explanation:

- `UPDATE wp_postmeta`: This specifies the table we want to modify - the `wp_postmeta` table.
- `SET meta_value = 0`: This defines the new value we want to set for the `meta_value` field.
- `WHERE post_id = 123`: This filters the update to affect only the post with ID 123.
- `AND meta_key = 'stock_count'`: This ensures we're updating the correct custom field named "stock_count".

2. **Execute the Query:** Run the update query. This will change the stock count for product ID 123 to 0.

- **Always back up your database before executing update queries.**
- Modify the queries based on your specific custom post type name, custom field names, and desired data manipulation.
- These are basic examples. You can explore more complex filtering, sorting, and data manipulation techniques using MySQL queries.

CHAPTER 8: LEVERAGING DATABASE VIEWS FOR SIMPLIFIED QUERIES

Learning Objectives: Understand and create database views for streamlined and reusable queries.

8.1 What are Database Views? Benefits and Use Cases for WordPress

Imagine a busy restaurant kitchen. Chefs rely on well-organized stations with specific ingredients readily available for different dishes. Database views in WordPress function similarly, offering a streamlined way to access and manage complex data queries.

Understanding Database Views:

A database view is a virtual table that doesn't store data itself. Instead, it acts as a pre-defined query that retrieves data from one or more underlying tables. Think of it like a recipe card in the kitchen – it references the ingredients (data) from the pantry (actual tables) but is not a physical container itself.

Benefits of Database Views in WordPress:

1. Simplification: Views can simplify complex queries, making them easier to understand, write, and maintain. Chefs don't

need to memorize every ingredient location in the pantry; they just follow the recipe card (view).
2. Security: You can control access to views, restricting sensitive data from direct manipulation. This is like having designated chefs handle specific ingredients to ensure proper use.
3. Performance: Well-designed views can improve query performance by pre-computing complex joins or filtering operations. It's like having pre-chopped ingredients ready for faster cooking.
4. Reusability: Views can be reused throughout your WordPress installation, reducing code redundancy and improving maintainability. Imagine using the same recipe card for multiple dishes.

Use Cases for Database Views in WordPress:

- ❖ Custom Reports: Create views to combine data from multiple tables for generating custom reports. For example, a view might combine user data with order data to show purchase history for specific user groups.
- ❖ Content Aggregation: Develop views to display specific content combinations on your website. This could involve showcasing recent blog posts from specific categories or authors.
- ❖ Data Security: Use views to restrict access to sensitive data within your database. You can create views that only expose necessary information for specific functionalities.

Example: A View for Recent Posts by Category

Let's consider a very common scenario where you want to display a list of the most recent posts from a specific category (e.g., "News") on your WordPress sidebar. Here's a simplified example of how a view can achieve this:

```sql
CREATE VIEW recent_news AS
SELECT p.ID, p.post_title, p.post_date
FROM wp_posts p
INNER JOIN wp_term_relationships tr ON p.ID = tr.object_id
INNER JOIN wp_terms t ON tr.term_taxonomy_id = t.term_id
WHERE t.slug = 'news'  -- Filter for posts in the "News" category
ORDER BY p.post_date DESC
LIMIT 5;  -- Show only the 5 most recent posts
```

Explanation:

This code creates a view named `recent_news`. It selects data (post ID, title, and date) from the `wp_posts` table (`p`) and joins it with two other tables:

`wp_term_relationships` (`tr`): This table links posts to categories.

`wp_terms` (`t`): This table stores information about categories, including their slug (used for filtering).

The `WHERE` clause filters for posts where the slug is "news," ensuring only posts from that category are included. The `ORDER BY` clause sorts the results by post date in descending order (most recent first). Finally, `LIMIT 5` restricts the view to display only the top 5 recent posts.

Using the View in Your Theme:

Once you've created the view, you can utilize it within your WordPress theme template to display the recent news posts. You can achieve this using standard WordPress functions to query the view and display the retrieved data.

- ❖ Database views require some understanding of SQL syntax.
- ❖ Consult your web hosting provider's documentation to ensure your server supports creating database views.
- ❖ Use views judiciously, as overly complex views can impact performance.

8.2 Creating and Managing Database Views for Common Queries

Database views in WordPress offer a powerful way to streamline complex data retrieval and simplify queries. This section dives into creating and managing views using phpMyAdmin, focusing on common use cases that can enhance your website's functionality.

Understanding Database Views:

Concept: A database view is a virtual table that acts as a pre-defined query, retrieving data from one or more underlying tables. Imagine it like a recipe card referencing ingredients from your pantry (actual tables) without being a physical container itself.

- **Benefits:**
- **Simplification:** Views make complex queries easier to understand, write, and maintain.
- **Security:** Control access to views, restricting sensitive data from direct manipulation.
- **Performance:** Well-designed views can improve query performance.
- **Reusability:** Reuse views throughout your WordPress installation for code maintainability.

Common Use Cases for Views in WordPress:

- **Custom Reports:** Combine data from multiple tables for reports (e.g., user data with order data for purchase history).
- **Content Aggregation:** Display specific content combinations (e.g., recent blog posts from a category or author).
- **Data Security:** Restrict access to sensitive data by creating views that expose only necessary information.

Creating a View with phpMyAdmin:

1. Access phpMyAdmin:
1. Use your web hosting service's login credentials (refer to Chapter 2.1 for guidance).
2. **Select Your Database:**
3. In the left-hand panel, locate your WordPress database and click on it to expand and reveal the tables.
4. **Create View Tab:**
5. Navigate to the "SQL" tab at the top of the phpMyAdmin interface. This is where you'll write and execute the SQL code for your view.
5. **Write the View Query:**
6. In the main text area, paste the SQL code for your desired view. Here are some examples with explanations:

Example 1: Recent Posts by Category

This view retrieves the most recent posts (5) from a specific category (e.g., "News").

SQL

```
CREATE VIEW recent_news AS
SELECT p.ID, p.post_title, p.post_date
FROM wp_posts p
INNER JOIN wp_term_relationships tr ON p.ID = tr.object_id
INNER JOIN wp_terms t ON tr.term_taxonomy_id = t.term_id
WHERE t.slug = 'news'   -- Filter for posts in the "News" category
ORDER BY p.post_date DESC
```

```
LIMIT 5;  -- Show only the 5 most recent posts
```

Explanation:

- This code creates a view named `recent_news`.
- It selects data (post ID, title, and date) from the `wp_posts` table (`p`).
- It joins with two other tables:
    - `wp_term_relationships` (`tr`) to link posts to categories.
    - `wp_terms` (`t`) to access category information (slug used for filtering).
- The `WHERE` clause ensures only posts from the "News" category (based on slug) are included.
- `ORDER BY` sorts results by post date (newest first).
- `LIMIT 5` restricts the view to display the top 5 recent posts.

Example 2: User Login History (Limited View for Security)

This view retrieves usernames and login timestamps, excluding passwords for security reasons.

SQL

```
CREATE VIEW recent_logins AS
SELECT u.user_login, l.login
FROM wp_users u
INNER JOIN wp_userlogin l ON u.ID = l.user_id
ORDER BY l.login DESC
LIMIT 10;  -- Show only the 10 most recent logins
```

Explanation:
- This view is named `recent_logins`.
- It selects user login names (`u.user_login`) and login timestamps (`l.login`) from the `wp_users` (`u`) and `wp_userlogin` (`l`) tables.
- Users and logins are linked based on user ID.
- Passwords are deliberately excluded for security.
- The results are ordered by login time (most recent first).
- `LIMIT 10` restricts the view to display the 10 most recent login attempts.

5. Execute the Query:
- Once you've reviewed your code for accuracy, click the "Go" button at the bottom of the page. phpMyAdmin will execute the query and create the view in your database.

Managing Views in phpMyAdmin:

Viewing Views: Views aren't displayed in the default table list. However, you can access them by expanding your database and looking for entries with the view icon (often a magnifying glass symbol). Clicking on a view name displays its definition (the SQL code used to create it).

Editing Views:

You can modify existing views by clicking on the "Edit" link next to the view name. This allows you to edit the SQL code defining the view and then save the changes.

Dropping Views:

If you no longer need a view, you can delete it by selecting the checkbox next to the view name and clicking the "Drop" button with the red "X" symbol at the bottom of the page. Use caution when dropping views, as it's permanent.

Security: Always back up your database before making significant changes, especially when creating or modifying views.

Testing: After creating a view, test it thoroughly within your WordPress environment to ensure it retrieves the intended data correctly.

Advanced Options: phpMyAdmin offers various options for creating views, including defining specific columns to be returned and specifying a check option (to ensure the view's data remains consistent). Refer to phpMyAdmin documentation for details on these advanced functionalities.

Additional Considerations:

Complexity: While these examples showcase basic views, you can create more intricate views involving multiple joins, aggregations (e.g., counting comments), and filtering conditions.

Performance: When working with complex views, consider potential performance implications on your website. Ensure the underlying queries are efficient and optimized.

Alternatives: In some cases, plugins might offer functionalities similar to views (e.g., custom reports). Evaluate if a plugin suits your needs before creating a view.

By understanding these concepts and following the steps outlined, you can leverage database views in WordPress to streamline data access, enhance security, and potentially improve the performance of your website's queries. Remember to start with simple views and gradually progress to more complex ones as you gain experience.

8.3 Using Views to Simplify Complex Data Retrieval Operations

Imagine you're managing a busy online store built with WordPress. Keeping track of inventory, orders, and customer data can involve complex queries across multiple database tables. Database views come to the rescue, acting as pre-defined queries that simplify these operations.

Understanding Database Views:

Concept: A database view is a virtual table that doesn't store data itself. Instead, it acts as a stored query, retrieving data from one or more underlying tables based on a defined criteria. Think of it like a saved search in your email client that automatically filters and displays specific messages.

Benefits of Using Views:
- **Simplification:** Views make complex data retrieval queries easier to write, understand, and maintain. You don't need to write the entire query every time you need that specific data set.
- **Security:** You can control access to views, restricting sensitive data from direct manipulation. This is like creating a view that only shows product names and prices, but not inventory levels (which might be confidential).
- **Performance:** Well-designed views can improve query performance by pre-computing complex joins or

filtering operations. Think of it like having a pre-filtered list of products ready for display, instead of searching through the entire inventory every time.
- **Reusability:** Views can be reused throughout your WordPress website, reducing code redundancy and improving maintainability. Just like a saved search in your email, you can reuse the view wherever you need that specific data set.

Using Views for Complex Data Retrieval:

Here's a scenario where a view can simplify a complex data retrieval operation:

Challenge: You want to display a list of recent orders for each customer on their account page. This requires joining the `wp_users` table with the `wp_posts` table (where post type is "shop_order") and the `wp_postmeta` table (to get order details).

Solution: Create a view that combines the necessary data from these tables. Here's an example SQL code for such a view:

SQL
```
CREATE VIEW customer_orders AS
SELECT u.user_login AS customer_name, p.ID AS order_id,
pm1.meta_value AS order_date, pm2.meta_value AS order_total
FROM wp_users u
```

```
INNER JOIN wp_posts p ON u.ID = p.post_author
INNER JOIN wp_postmeta pm1 ON p.ID = pm1.post_id AND
pm1.meta_key = 'order_date'
INNER JOIN wp_postmeta pm2 ON p.ID = pm2.post_id AND
pm2.meta_key = 'order_total'
WHERE p.post_type = 'shop_order';
```

Explanation:

- This view is named `customer_orders`.
- It selects customer login name (`u.user_login`), order ID (`p.ID`), order date (`pm1.meta_value`), and order total (`pm2.meta_value`) from relevant tables.
- Joins are used to connect user data with orders and order details stored as meta data.
- The `WHERE` clause ensures only posts of type "shop_order" (representing orders) are included.

Using the View in Your Theme:

Once you've created the view, you can utilize it within your WordPress theme template to display customer orders. You can achieve this using standard WordPress functions to query the view and display the retrieved data for each user.

Remember:

- Database views require some understanding of SQL syntax.

- Consult your web hosting provider's documentation to ensure your server supports creating database views.
- Use views judiciously, as overly complex views can impact performance.

Project: Create a database view for a frequently used complex query in your WordPress environment.

Database views offer a powerful mechanism to simplify complex queries in WordPress. This project guides you through creating a view for a frequently used complex query in your specific WordPress environment.

Identifying a Suitable Query:
- Reflect on your WordPress website. Are there any complex queries you use frequently within themes, plugins, or custom code?
- Look for queries that involve multiple table joins, filtering conditions, or aggregations (e.g., counting comments).
- Here are some common scenarios where views can be beneficial:
    - **User Reports:** Combining user data with order data to analyze purchase history for specific user groups.

- **Content Performance:** Joining posts with comments tables to identify top-rated content based on average ratings or comment counts.
- **Product Listings:** Filtering and sorting product data from multiple custom tables based on various criteria (e.g., category, price range, stock availability).

Choosing Your Query:

- Select a complex query you use frequently and would benefit from simplification through a view.
- Ensure you understand the logic and purpose of the chosen query.

Example Scenario: Top-Rated Posts with Multiple Joins

Let's consider a scenario where you want to create a view to display the top 5 rated posts on your blog, along with their average rating and total comment count. This would involve joining multiple tables and performing aggregation functions (average rating).

Steps to Create the View:

1. **Access phpMyAdmin:**
   - Use your web hosting service's login credentials (refer to Chapter 2.1 for guidance).
2. **Select Your Database:**

- In the left-hand panel, locate your WordPress database and click on it to expand and reveal the tables.

3. **Create View Tab:**
- Navigate to the "SQL" tab at the top of the phpMyAdmin interface. This is where you'll write and execute the SQL code for your view.

4. **Write the View Query:**
- In the main text area, paste the SQL code for your view. Here's an example for the top-rated posts scenario:

SQL
```
CREATE VIEW top_rated_posts AS
SELECT p.ID, p.post_title,
AVG(r.rating) AS average_rating, COUNT(c.comment_ID) AS comment_count
FROM wp_posts p
INNER JOIN wp_comments c ON p.ID = c.comment_post_ID
INNER JOIN wp_commentmeta r ON c.comment_ID = r.comment_id
WHERE r.meta_key = 'rating'  -- Filter for comments with "rating" meta key
GROUP BY p.ID
ORDER BY average_rating DESC
LIMIT 5;
```

Explanation:
- This code creates a view named `top_rated_posts`.
- It selects data from three tables:
    - `wp_posts` (p): Contains post information (ID and title).
    - `wp_comments` (c): Stores information about comments (linked to posts by `comment_post_ID`).
    - `wp_commentmeta` (r): Holds comment meta data, including ratings (identified by `meta_key` "rating").
- The `INNER JOIN` clauses connect the tables based on post ID and comment ID.
- The `WHERE` clause ensures only comments with a "rating" meta key are considered.
- `GROUP BY p.ID` groups the data by post ID for accurate average rating and comment count per post.
- `AVG(r.rating)` calculates the average rating for each post.
- `COUNT(c.comment_ID)` counts the total comments for each post.
- Finally, the results are ordered by `average_rating` in descending order (highest rated first) and limited to the top 5 posts using `LIMIT 5`.

5. **Execute the Query:**

Once you've reviewed your code for accuracy, click the "Go" button at the bottom of the page. phpMyAdmin will execute the query and create the view in your database.

Using the View in Your WordPress Theme:

Now that you have created the view, you can utilize it within your WordPress theme template to display the top-rated posts. Standard WordPress functions allow you to query the view and display the retrieved data (post title, average rating, comment count).

Remember:

- ❖ Adapt the example view query to match your specific complex query and table structure.
- ❖ Always back up your database before creating or modifying views.
- ❖ Test the view thoroughly within your WordPress environment to ensure it functions as expected.

CHAPTER 9: SECURITY CONSIDERATIONS FOR DATABASE ACCESS

Learning Objectives: Implement essential security practices to protect your WordPress database.

Your WordPress website's database holds valuable information – posts, user data, comments, and configurations. Just like securing your home, safeguarding your database is paramount. This chapter explores essential security measures to protect your database from unauthorized access and potential threats.

Understanding Database Security Threats:

- **Hacking Attempts:** Malicious actors might try to gain unauthorized access to your database to steal sensitive information, inject malware, or disrupt your website's functionality.
- **Data Breaches:** Security vulnerabilities or human error can expose your database, leading to data breaches where unauthorized users access confidential information.
- **SQL Injection Attacks**: These attacks exploit vulnerabilities in code that processes user input. Hackers can inject malicious SQL code into forms or queries, potentially manipulating or stealing data.

Securing Your WordPress Database:

Here are some key strategies to fortify your database security:

1. **Strong Login Credentials:**

Use complex passwords: Avoid using dictionary words, personal information, or easily guessable patterns. Leverage a password manager to generate and store strong, unique passwords for your WordPress login and database access.

Enable Two-Factor Authentication (2FA): This adds an extra layer of security by requiring a second verification code (e.g., from your phone) in addition to your password when logging in.

2. **Limit User Access:**

User Roles and Permissions: WordPress offers various user roles (administrator, editor, author, etc.) with different access levels. Assign users the minimum level of access required for their roles. This minimizes the potential damage if a user account is compromised.

Database User Permissions: Within your database management system (often phpMyAdmin), restrict access to the database itself. Create separate database user accounts with limited privileges for specific purposes (e.g., a user for your WordPress installation with read-write access only to the WordPress tables). Avoid using the root user account for everyday tasks.

3. **Keep WordPress and Plugins Updated:**

Regular Updates: Outdated WordPress versions and plugins can contain security vulnerabilities. Regularly update WordPress core, themes, and plugins to address known security issues and patch vulnerabilities that hackers might exploit.

Security Plugins: Consider using reputable security plugins that offer features like login attempt monitoring, malware scanning, and firewalls to add an extra layer of protection.

4. Database Backups:

Regular Backups: Regularly backing up your database ensures you have a recent copy in case of data loss due to accidental deletion, security breaches, or hardware failures. You can use plugins or schedule automated backups through your web hosting provider.

Secure Backup Storage: Don't store backups on the same server as your website. Consider storing them on a separate server or cloud storage service to ensure they remain accessible even if your website is compromised.

5. Secure Development Practices:

Input Validation: Always validate and sanitize user input before using it in database queries. This helps prevent SQL injection attacks where malicious code might be injected through forms or user-submitted data. Here are some resources on input validation techniques in PHP: https://www.geeksforgeeks.org/how-to-read-user-or-console-input-in-php/

Use Prepared Statements: Prepared statements help prevent SQL injection vulnerabilities by separating the SQL code from the data. The database server prepares and validates the SQL statement before executing it with the provided data. Here are some resources on prepared statements in PHP with MySQLi: https://www.php.net/manual/en/mysqli.quickstart.prepared-statements.php

Additional Security Considerations:

Secure Web Hosting: Choose a web hosting provider with a strong security track record. Look for features like firewalls, intrusion detection systems, and regular security audits.

Database Encryption: Some database management systems offer encryption capabilities to further protect sensitive data at rest (stored on the server). Consult your web hosting provider or database documentation for details on available encryption options.

9.1 Understanding User Privileges and Access Control in MySQL

Within your WordPress database, a crucial security aspect is managing user access and privileges. This section dives into understanding the core concepts of MySQL user accounts and how to control what data they can access and modify.

Understanding MySQL Users:

Concept: A MySQL user is an account that grants access to a MySQL server and potentially specific databases or tables within that server. Imagine a library – librarian accounts grant access to the library (server) with varying permission levels (depending on the user type – administrator, patron, etc.) for borrowing or managing resources (databases and tables).

User Privileges: These define what actions a user can perform on the database server. Common privileges include selecting data (READ), inserting new data (CREATE), updating existing data (UPDATE), and deleting data (DELETE).

Types of MySQL Users:

Global Users: These users have access to the MySQL server itself and can potentially manage all databases on the server. This is a powerful privilege and should be assigned with caution, typically only to system administrators.

Database Users: These users have access to specific databases on the MySQL server. They can be granted privileges to perform various operations (SELECT, CREATE, UPDATE, DELETE) on specific tables within those databases. This is the most common scenario for WordPress installations, where a dedicated user is created for WordPress to access its tables.

Granting and Revoking Privileges:

GRANT statement: This is used to assign specific privileges to a MySQL user. The syntax involves specifying the user, the privileges being granted (e.g., SELECT, ALL PRIVILEGES), and optionally, the database or table the privileges apply to.

REVOKE statement: This is used to remove previously granted privileges from a MySQL user. The syntax is similar to GRANT, specifying the user and the privileges to be revoked.

Securing Your WordPress with User Privileges:

Principle of Least Privilege: Grant users only the minimum level of access required for their tasks. For WordPress, a dedicated user with SELECT, CREATE, UPDATE, and DELETE privileges on the WordPress tables is typically sufficient. Avoid granting unnecessary privileges like DROP (to delete tables) or global privileges that could compromise the database server.

Separate User Accounts: Don't use the same user account for both WordPress and administrative tasks on the MySQL server. This creates an additional layer of security in case one account's credentials are compromised.

Here's an example (without revealing actual passwords) demonstrating how to create a separate user for your WordPress installation and grant it the necessary privileges:

```sql
CREATE USER 'wp_user'@'localhost' IDENTIFIED BY 'your_strong_password'; -- Create a user for WordPress with a strong password

GRANT SELECT, CREATE, UPDATE, DELETE ON `wp_database`. TO 'wp_user'@'localhost'; -- Grant privileges on all tables within the 'wp_database' for the 'wp_user'

FLUSH PRIVILEGES; -- Apply the changes
```

Remember:

Replace 'your_strong_password' with an actual strong password.

Replace 'wp_database' with the actual name of your WordPress database.

This is a basic example. Consult your web hosting provider's documentation or MySQL documentation for more advanced privilege management options.

9.2 Securing Your Database Connection: Best Practices for Usernames and Passwords

Your WordPress website's database stores critical information – posts, user data, comments, and configurations. Protecting this data from unauthorized access is paramount. A secure database connection hinges on robust usernames and passwords. This section dives into best practices for creating and managing these credentials to safeguard your website.

Understanding Database Credentials:

Database User: A database user account grants access to the database. Think of it like a key that unlocks a specific door (database).

Username: A unique identifier for the database user account.

Password: A secret code used in conjunction with the username for authentication. Only authorized users with the correct credentials can access the database.

Why Strong Credentials Matter:

Weak credentials like dictionary words or predictable patterns are easy for hackers to guess or crack using automated tools. This can lead to unauthorized access and potential data breaches.

Strong credentials make it significantly harder for attackers to gain access, safeguarding your valuable database information.

Best Practices for Secure Database Credentials:

1. **Use Complex Passwords:**

Length is key: Aim for passwords at least 12 characters long.

Diversity is essential: Combine uppercase and lowercase letters, numbers, and symbols (@, $, %, etc.) in your passwords.

Avoid patterns: Steer clear of easily guessable patterns like keyboard sequences (123456) or personal information (birthdates, names).

Password Managers: Consider using a reputable password manager to generate and store strong, unique passwords for all your accounts, including your database user.

2. **Avoid Default Credentials:**

Many web hosting providers set up databases with default usernames (e.g., "root") and passwords. Always change these defaults to unique and complex credentials.

3. **Limit User Privileges:**

Principle of least privilege: Grant database user accounts only the minimum level of access required for their specific purpose. For instance, a WordPress installation might have a user with read-write access only to its tables, not general administrative privileges.

4. **Rotate Passwords Regularly:**

Regularly change your database user passwords (e.g., every few months). This reduces the risk of compromise even if a password is somehow exposed.

Strong Password Examples:

These are examples of strong passwords (avoid using these exact ones for your own security):

`Th1s_is@Str0ngPa$$w0rd!`

`InclUde$ymbols&Numbers?`

`Ch@ngeM3R3gularly`

Remember:

Never share your database credentials: These credentials are confidential and should not be shared with anyone who doesn't require direct database access.

Beware of phishing attempts: Phishing emails or websites might try to trick you into revealing your database credentials. Be cautious about any requests for login information.

By following these best practices, you can significantly strengthen your database security and make it much harder for unauthorized users to gain access to your WordPress website's sensitive data.

9.3 Ongoing Maintenance: Keeping Your WordPress Database Secure

Securing your WordPress database is not a one-time fix; it's an ongoing process that requires vigilance and regular maintenance. Here are key strategies to keep your database defenses strong:

1. Stay Updated:

WordPress Core, Themes, and Plugins: As mentioned previously, outdated software can harbor vulnerabilities. Set up automatic updates whenever possible to ensure your WordPress core, themes, and plugins are always on the latest secure versions.

Security Software Updates: If you're using security plugins, keep them updated as well. Security researchers constantly discover new threats, and security plugins are updated to address these evolving risks.

2. Monitor and Manage User Activity:

User Login Attempts: Consider using security plugins that monitor login attempts. This can help you detect potential brute-force attacks where hackers try to guess passwords automatically. You can set up alerts or implement mechanisms to block suspicious login attempts after a certain number of failed tries.

User Roles and Permissions: Regularly review user roles and permissions. Revoke access for inactive users and ensure user privileges are aligned with their current roles.

3. Secure Your Development Environment:

Development and Staging Sites: If you develop or test customizations on a development or staging site, ensure those environments are secure as well. These environments can be inadvertently left with vulnerabilities that could potentially be exploited to gain access to your main website's database.

Secure Coding Practices: For developers, stay updated on secure coding practices and common vulnerabilities specific to WordPress development. Here are some resources to get you started:

WordPress Security Development Kit (SDK): https://wordpress.org/about/security/

OWASP Top 10 Web Application Security Risks: https://owasp.org/www-project-top-ten/

4. Maintain Strong Backups:

Regular Backups: Continue to perform regular database backups. How often you back up depends on how frequently your data changes. If your site updates frequently, consider more frequent backups.

Test Backups: Don't assume your backups are functional until you test them! Restore a backup to a staging site or test environment periodically to ensure you can recover your data if needed.

Secure Backup Storage: Store backups securely off-site, preferably in a cloud storage service with strong security measures. This ensures your backups remain accessible even if your web server is compromised.

5. Stay Informed:

Security News and Updates: Subscribe to security blogs or resources from reputable WordPress security plugin providers. Staying informed about new threats and vulnerabilities allows you to take proactive measures to protect your website.

WordPress Community: The WordPress community is a valuable resource. Participate in forums and discussions to learn from other users' experiences and stay updated on security best practices.

Security is an ongoing process. By following these recommendations and staying informed, you can significantly reduce the risk of database breaches and protect your WordPress website's valuable data.

Chapter 10: Advanced Techniques and Resources for WordPress Database Optimization

Building upon the foundational concepts covered in Chapter 9, this chapter explores advanced techniques and resources to optimize your WordPress database for peak performance. While the previous chapter focused on general website performance optimization strategies, here we delve deeper into the database itself, exploring methods to streamline queries and ensure efficient data storage and retrieval.

Understanding Database Optimization Needs:

Database Impact on Performance: A well-optimized database can significantly improve website speed. Conversely, an unoptimized database with bloated tables, redundant data, and inefficient queries can lead to sluggish performance.

Focus on Queries: Database optimization often centers around optimizing queries – the instructions that retrieve data from your database. Inefficient queries can strain your server's resources and slow down page load times.

Advanced Database Optimization Techniques:

1. **Database Normalization:**

Concept: Database normalization is a process of organizing your database tables to minimize redundancy and improve data integrity. It involves structuring tables to avoid storing the same data in multiple places, reducing storage requirements and simplifying queries.

2. Indexing:

Indexes: Indexes are like reference lists in a book, allowing the database to quickly locate specific data within a table. Properly designed indexes can significantly speed up queries that search for specific data.

Identifying Indexing Needs: Analyze your most frequent queries to identify which table columns are used for filtering or sorting data. These columns are prime candidates for creating indexes.

3. Query Optimization:

Understanding Queries: Familiarize yourself with the basics of SQL, the language used to interact with relational databases like the one used by WordPress. This knowledge empowers you to analyze and optimize queries for efficiency.

Caching Queries: Consider caching the results of frequently executed queries to reduce the load on your database server. However, be mindful of data freshness; implement mechanisms to refresh the cache periodically if the underlying data changes frequently.

Plugins for Optimization: Several WordPress plugins offer database optimization functionalities. These plugins can help identify bloated tables, optimize queries, and even automate some optimization tasks. However, use these plugins with caution and always back up your database before running any optimization routines.

Advanced Resources for Database Optimization:

MySQL Documentation: The official MySQL documentation is a comprehensive resource for learning about database management, query optimization, and advanced functionalities: https://dev.mysql.com/doc/

Performance Profiling Tools: Utilize profiling tools to identify bottlenecks in your database queries. These tools can pinpoint slow queries and help you understand how to optimize them. Popular options include phpMyAdmin's query statistics and Query Monitor plugins.

Database Management Experts: For complex optimization needs, consider consulting with database management experts. They possess in-depth knowledge and experience in optimizing databases for performance.

Remember:

Advanced database optimization techniques require a solid understanding of database concepts and potentially some SQL knowledge. If you're a beginner, it's recommended to start with the basic optimization techniques covered in Chapter 9 and gradually progress to more advanced strategies as you gain experience. Always prioritize creating a full backup of your database before attempting any significant optimization procedures.

Important Considerations for Advanced Techniques:

Testing is Crucial: Before implementing any advanced optimization techniques, thoroughly test your website in a staging environment (a copy of your live site used for testing). This helps ensure that the changes don't introduce unexpected issues or break functionalities on your live website.

Database Backups are Essential: Always create a complete backup of your database before running any optimization routines, especially when dealing with advanced techniques. This allows you to revert to a previous state if something goes wrong during the optimization process.

Security Implications: Be mindful of potential security implications when using certain optimization techniques. For instance, caching database queries might require additional security measures to prevent unauthorized access to cached data. Consult with a security expert if unsure about the security implications of specific techniques.

Denormalization: While database normalization is generally recommended, there can be situations where controlled denormalization (introducing some redundancy) can improve performance for specific queries. This is an advanced technique that requires careful consideration and understanding of the trade-offs involved.

Database Sharding: For very large and high-traffic websites, database sharding might be considered. Sharding involves distributing your database across multiple servers to handle the increased load and improve scalability. However, database sharding is a complex process that requires significant expertise to implement and manage effectively.

CHAPTER 11: Performance Optimization Beyond the Database:

We've explored various techniques to optimize your WordPress database for peak performance. However, database optimization is just one piece of the puzzle. This chapter dives into additional strategies to enhance your website's overall speed, ensuring a smooth and fast user experience.

Understanding Website Performance:

Factors Affecting Performance: Several elements can impact website speed, including server resources, image size, the number of plugins, and inefficient code. Optimizing these aspects can significantly improve website performance.

Optimizing Beyond the Database:

Here are key areas to focus on for performance optimization beyond the database:

1. Server-Side Caching:

Have you ever wondered how some websites load lightning fast, even with complex content? One secret weapon is server-side caching. In this chapter, we'll explore server-side caching for WordPress, a powerful technique to significantly improve website performance.

What is Server-Side Caching?

Concept: Server-side caching involves storing a temporary copy of a fully rendered webpage on the server itself. When a user visits the website, the server can deliver this cached version instead of having to regenerate the entire page dynamically every time. This significantly reduces server load and page load times for visitors.

Benefits of Server-Side Caching:
- Faster Loading Times: By serving cached pages, your website can load significantly faster for visitors, enhancing user experience and potentially improving search engine ranking.
- Reduced Server Load: Server-side caching alleviates the burden on your server by minimizing the need to process the same page requests repeatedly. This can be particularly beneficial for high-traffic websites.
- Improved Scalability: With server-side caching, your website can handle more traffic efficiently by serving pre-cached content. This allows your website to scale better as your audience grows.

How Does Server-Side Caching Work?

1. Initial Visit: When a user visits your website for the first time, WordPress generates the webpage dynamically using PHP and retrieves data from the database. This fully rendered webpage is then sent to the user's browser for display.

2. Caching the Page: If server-side caching is enabled, the server creates a cached copy of the entire

rendered webpage (HTML content) and stores it on the server's local storage (usually hard disk or RAM).

3. Subsequent Visits: When another user visits the same page, the server checks its cache. If a cached version of the page exists and is still valid (not expired), the server retrieves the cached copy and delivers it to the user's browser instead of re-generating the page dynamically.

Important to Note:

Server-side caching typically works best for static content that doesn't change frequently. For dynamic content like user login pages or shopping carts, caching might need to be more granular to exclude specific elements that require updates on every visit.

Enabling Server-Side Caching:

The specific steps for enabling server-side caching can vary depending on your web hosting provider. Here's a general approach:

1. Check your hosting provider's documentation. Many web hosting providers offer server-side caching as a built-in feature or through their control panel.

2. Look for options related to caching or website optimization. Enable the server-side caching functionality.

3. Configure caching settings (optional). Some hosting providers might offer options to control caching behavior, such as setting cache expiration times.

Additional Considerations:

Caching Plugins: While some hosting providers offer built-in server-side caching, you can also use caching plugins for WordPress. These plugins provide additional features and configuration options for managing your website's caching behavior.

Cache Invalidation: It's important to consider how your website updates cached pages when the content changes. Some caching mechanisms automatically invalidate (remove) outdated cached versions when the source content is modified. For others, you might need to implement manual invalidation mechanisms.

Server-side caching is a powerful tool to significantly improve the performance of your WordPress website. By implementing this technique, you can ensure a faster and more responsive user experience for your visitors. Remember to consult your web hosting provider's documentation for specific instructions on enabling server-side caching on your website.

Caching Mechanisms: Many web hosting providers offer server-side caching solutions. Additionally, popular caching plugins can be used to implement caching functionalities on your WordPress website. These plugins can cache entire pages, database queries, or specific objects.

11.2 Code Optimization:
Just like a well-oiled machine, efficient code plays a crucial role in a fast-loading WordPress website. Optimized code ensures your website runs smoothly and delivers information to your visitors quickly. This chapter explores key strategies to streamline your WordPress website's code for optimal performance.

Understanding Code Optimization:

Impact on Performance: Inefficient code can significantly slow down your website. This can involve bulky code files, unnecessary elements, or code written in a way that requires more processing power from the server.

Focus on Efficiency: Code optimization aims to make your website's code leaner and more efficient. This improves website responsiveness and enhances the user experience.

Optimizing Your WordPress Code:

Here are some key strategies to optimize your WordPress code:

1. Minification:

Concept: Minification involves removing unnecessary characters (spaces, comments, line breaks) from your website's code (HTML, CSS, JavaScript). This reduces file sizes without affecting functionality and can lead to faster loading times.

Implementation: Several methods exist for minifying code.

Manual Minification: While not recommended for large websites, you can manually remove unnecessary characters from your code files using a text editor.

Minification Plugins: Many WordPress plugins offer minification functionalities. These plugins can automatically minify your code during page load or create minified versions of your code files for future use.

2. Code Splitting:

Concept: Code splitting involves breaking down large code files (e.g., a massive JavaScript file) into smaller, more manageable chunks. This allows the browser to load only the code required for the initial page view, improving perceived performance. Users won't have to wait for the entire script to download before seeing the content.

Implementation: Code splitting techniques can be implemented manually or with the help of bundlers like Webpack or Parcel. These tools automate code splitting and other optimization tasks.

3. Leverage Browser Caching:

Concept: Browser caching allows your website's static resources (CSS, JavaScript files, images) to be stored locally on the visitor's device. This way, the browser doesn't need to download these files again on subsequent visits to the same pages, improving loading speeds.

Implementation: Most WordPress caching plugins offer options to configure browser caching for your website's static resources. You can also set caching headers manually in your server configuration.

4. Database Optimization:

Reduced Database Calls: While covered in a previous chapter, it's worth reiterating that optimizing your database can have a significant impact on code efficiency. Streamlined queries and a well-structured database reduce the load on your server and improve page load times.

5. Lazy Loading:

Concept: Lazy loading defers the loading of non-critical content (like images or videos below the fold) until the user scrolls down to that section of the page. This prioritizes loading the content immediately visible to the user, improving the initial page load time.

Implementation: Several JavaScript libraries and WordPress plugins offer lazy loading functionalities. These tools can automatically detect and defer the loading of non-essential content.

Additional Code Optimization Tips:

Avoid Inline Styles and Scripts: Embedding styles and scripts directly within your HTML code can clutter your code and make it harder to maintain. It's generally recommended to use separate CSS and JavaScript files.

Optimize Images: As mentioned previously, large image files can significantly slow down your website. Use tools to compress images without sacrificing quality. Consider using next-gen image formats like WebP if supported by your hosting provider.

Minimize HTTP Requests: The more HTTP requests your website makes (e.g., to load images, fonts, stylesheets), the slower it can load. Combine files (e.g., CSS sprites for multiple small images) and minimize the number of external resources whenever possible.

Remember:

Code optimization is an ongoing process. Regularly monitor your website's performance and experiment with different techniques to find the best combination for your website's specific needs. By implementing these strategies, you can create leaner, more efficient code that contributes to a faster and more user-friendly website experience.

Minification: Code minification involves removing unnecessary characters (whitespace, comments) from your website's HTML, CSS, and JavaScript files. This reduces file size and improves loading speeds. Minification can be achieved through plugins or online tools.

Optimizing Code Delivery: Consider techniques like code splitting (loading critical code first) and asynchronous loading (loading non-critical scripts without blocking page rendering) to optimize how your website delivers code to the browser.

11.3 Image Optimization:

Images are essential for enhancing your website's visual appeal and user experience. However, large, unoptimized images can significantly slow down your website's loading speed. This chapter dives into image optimization techniques specifically tailored for WordPress websites.

Understanding Image Optimization:

File Size vs. Quality: Image optimization aims to reduce the file size of an image without sacrificing too much visual quality. Smaller file sizes translate to faster loading times for your website.

Common Image Formats: There are various image formats commonly used on websites. Each format has its strengths and weaknesses:

JPEG (Joint Photographic Experts Group): Ideal for photographs with a wide range of colors. JPEG uses compression techniques that can reduce file size significantly, but with some potential loss of quality at higher compression levels.

PNG (Portable Network Graphic): Suitable for graphics with sharp edges and transparent backgrounds (e.g., logos, icons). PNG offers lossless compression, meaning the image quality remains intact, but file sizes can be larger compared to JPEG for photographs.

GIF (Graphics Interchange Format): Limited to a maximum of 256 colors, making it suitable for simple graphics or animations. GIFs can also support transparency.

Optimizing Images for WordPress:

Here are some key strategies to optimize images for your WordPress website:

1. **Choose the Right Format**:

Photos: Use JPEG format for photographs.

Graphics and Icons: Use PNG format for graphics and icons with sharp edges or transparent backgrounds.

Simple Animations: Consider GIF format for simple animations, but be mindful of file size limitations.

2. Resize Images:

Don't upload high-resolution images: Only upload images sized for the dimensions they will be displayed on your website. There's no point in loading a large image if it's only shown as a thumbnail. Use an image editing software or online tools to resize images before uploading them to WordPress.

3. Compression Tools:

Lossless vs. Lossy Compression: Several online tools and WordPress plugins offer image compression functionalities. Some use lossless compression, which reduces file size without affecting quality (but the reduction might be minimal). Others use lossy compression, which can significantly reduce file size but with some potential quality loss. Experiment with different tools and compression levels to find the best balance between file size and acceptable quality for your images.

4. Lazy Loading:

Prioritize Above-the-Fold Content: Consider implementing lazy loading for images below the fold (not visible initially when the page loads). This delays loading non-critical images until the user scrolls down to that section, improving the initial page load time. Many WordPress themes and plugins offer lazy loading functionality.

Additional Tips:

Optimize Image Metadata: Remove unnecessary metadata (information embedded within the image file) that might contribute to file size.

Serve Images Efficiently: Utilize a Content Delivery Network (CDN) to store and deliver your images from geographically distributed servers, potentially improving loading times for visitors in different locations.

Image optimization is an ongoing process. By implementing these strategies, you can significantly reduce image file sizes and ensure your WordPress website loads quickly, providing a better user experience for your visitors.

Image Size and Format: Large image files can significantly slow down your website. Use tools to compress images without sacrificing too much quality. Choose appropriate formats: JPEG for photos and PNG for graphics with sharp edges and transparent backgrounds.

Image Dimensions: Resize images to the exact dimensions displayed on your website. There's no point in loading a high-resolution image if it's only displayed as a thumbnail.

Content Delivery Network (CDN):

In our quest for a speedy website, we've explored various optimization techniques. Let's delve into a powerful tool called a Content Delivery Network (CDN) that can significantly boost your WordPress website's performance, especially for geographically dispersed visitors.

What is a Content Delivery Network (CDN)?

Imagine a network of servers strategically located around the globe, each containing cached copies of your website's static content (images, JavaScript, CSS). When a user visits your website, their request is directed to the nearest CDN server. This server delivers the static content much faster than if it had to travel from your original web server, which might be located far away.

- **Benefits of Using a CDN:**
- Faster Loading Times: By serving content from geographically closer servers, CDNs significantly reduce load times for visitors, especially those in locations distant from your primary server. This translates to a smoother user experience and potentially improved bounce rates (visitors leaving your site due to slow loading).
- Improved Scalability: CDNs can handle sudden traffic spikes more effectively than a single web server. They distribute the load across their network, ensuring your website remains accessible even during high-traffic periods.

- Reduced Server Load: Offloading static content delivery to a CDN frees up resources on your web server, allowing it to focus on handling dynamic content (like processing user interactions or database queries).

How Does a CDN Work with WordPress?

1. Setting Up a CDN: Sign up for a CDN service provider and configure your domain name to work with the CDN.

2. CDN Fetches Content: The CDN fetches static content (images, CSS, JavaScript) from your origin server (your web server) and stores cached copies on its edge servers around the world.

3. Visitor Requests Content: When a visitor accesses your website, their request is routed to the nearest CDN server based on their location.

4. CDN Delivers Content: The CDN server delivers the cached static content to the visitor's browser, significantly faster than if it came from your original server.

Things to Consider When Using a CDN:

CDN Pricing: CDN pricing structures can vary. Some offer pay-as-you-go models, while others have fixed monthly fees. Choose a plan that aligns with your website's traffic and budget.

Content Caching Rules: Most CDNs allow you to configure caching rules to determine how long specific content should be cached before refreshing from your origin server. This is important for content that changes frequently (e.g., news articles).

Integration with WordPress: Many popular CDN providers offer plugins that simplify integration with your WordPress website. These plugins can automate tasks like configuring your CDN and managing cached content.

Popular CDN Providers:

There are several reputable CDN providers available, each with its own features and pricing plans. Here are a few well-known options:

CloudFlare: https://www.cloudflare.com/

Amazon CloudFront: https://aws.amazon.com/cloudfront/

Google Cloud CDN: https://cloud.google.com/storage

Fastly: https://www.fastly.com/

A CDN can be a valuable asset for any website, especially those with a global audience. By implementing a CDN, you can significantly improve website performance, enhance user experience, and potentially boost your website's search engine ranking (faster websites tend to rank higher). Carefully evaluate your website's needs and choose a CDN provider that offers the right features and pricing structure for you.

CDN Benefits: A CDN is a network of geographically distributed servers that store copies of your website's static content (images, JavaScript, CSS). When a user visits your website, the content is served from the nearest CDN server, reducing load times for visitors in different locations.

Additional Performance Tips:

Browser Caching: Configure your website to leverage browser caching for static elements. This allows browsers to store frequently accessed files locally, reducing the need to download them again on subsequent visits.

Minimize HTTP Requests: The more HTTP requests your website makes (e.g., to load images, fonts, stylesheets), the slower it can load. Combine files (e.g., CSS sprites for multiple small images) and minimize the number of external resources whenever possible.

Lazy Loading: Consider implementing lazy loading for images or other content below the fold (not visible initially when the page loads). This delays loading non-critical content until the user scrolls down to that section, improving the initial page load time.

Monitoring and Testing:

Website Speed Testing Tools: Use website speed testing tools like Google PageSpeed Insights (https://developers.google.com/speed/docs/insights/v5/about) to identify areas for improvement.

Test and Measure: Experiment with different optimization techniques and measure the impact on your website's speed. This helps you identify the most effective solutions for your specific website.

www.ingramcontent.com/pod-product-compliance
Lightning Source LLC
Chambersburg PA
CBHW062105220526
45471CB00010B/3604